PILLOW SELF-TALK

5 MINUTES BEFORE BED TO START LIVING THE LIFE OF YOUR DREAMS

KRISTEN HELMSTETTER

Green
Butterfly
Press

~

VI.4

ABOUT THE AUTHOR

In 2018, Kristen Helmstetter sold everything to travel the world with her husband and daughter. She currently splits her time between Florida and a medieval hilltop town in Umbria, Italy.

She writes romance novels under the pen name Brisa Starr.

Listen to *Coffee Self-Talk with Kristen Helmstetter* wherever you listen to podcasts.

You can also find her on Instagram:

 instagram.com/coffeeselftalk

OTHER BOOKS BY KRISTEN HELMSTETTER

Coffee Self-Talk: 5 Minutes a Day to Start Living Your Magical Life

The Coffee Self-Talk Starter Pages: A Quick Daily Workbook to Jumpstart Your Coffee Self-Talk

The Coffee Self-Talk Daily Reader #1 & #2: Bite-Sized Nuggets of Magic to Add to Your Morning Routine

Wine Self-Talk: 15 Minutes to Relax & Tap Into Your Inner Genius

The Coffee Self-Talk Guided Journal: Writing Prompts & Inspiration for Living Your Magical Life

Tea Time Self-Talk: A Little Afternoon Bliss for Living Your Magical Life

Coffee Self-Talk for Dudes: 5 Minutes a Day to Start Living Your Legendary Life

Coffee Self-Talk for Teen Girls: 5 Minutes a Day for Confidence, Achievement & Lifelong Happiness

The Coffee Self-Talk for Teen Girls Guided Journal: Writing Prompts & Inspiration for Girls in High School

This book is dedicated to my husband.

Thank you for being such an amazing man, my handsome night owl, my guardian in the night.

~

If I could reach up and hold a star for every time you made me smile, I would have the whole night sky in the palm of my hand.

— UNKNOWN

CONTENTS

MAGICAL LIVING & SPIRITUALITY

LUMINOUS HEALTH, HEALING & LONGEVITY

CELESTIAL SURRENDER & PEACE

ETERNAL HAPPINESS

INTRODUCTION

Dear Friend,

I'm thrilled you're joining me on this adventure to live the life of your dreams and manifest your heartfelt desires using *Pillow Self-Talk*. Welcome! Grab yourself a cup of relaxing chamomile tea if you'd like, and let's dive in.

A year ago, I wrote a book called *Coffee Self-Talk*, in which I shared a simple but profound process for how you can take five minutes a day, with your delicious cup of coffee, and start living a magical life. In that book, I described how my life had looked fine on paper—my family had love, health, and success—but something was missing. My life lacked purpose. It lacked sparkle. There was no shine, no *magic*. That is, until I started doing my daily Coffee Self-Talk ritual, and then... BAM! Everything changed, in just a few days.

As of this writing, over a hundred thousand people have that book. Many of them write to me, and they often ask if I have a self-talk routine for bedtime.

It just so happens, I do. I call it *Pillow Self-Talk*. I use it to wind down my days. It's my favorite way to chill my mind and relax into a state of bliss, so I can easily fall asleep, dream magical dreams, and wake up feeling amazing and ready to take on the world. Doing this special ritual every night aligns my heart and mind to help me continue manifesting my life and dreams, even though I'm asleep.

Pillow Self-Talk is similar to *Coffee Self-Talk*, in that you use amazing self-talk to rewire your brain for living a magical life. But I've modified Pillow Self-Talk to come at the opposite end of the day. It's during this special time, bedtime, where you'll discover how to take advantage of the last minutes before falling asleep to help you make your dreams come true. And your brain gets busy rewiring itself, into a brain that can make your dreams come true, literally while you sleep.

Think of these two forms of self-talk—*coffee* and *pillow*—as two bookends to your day. By creating a specific ritual for your self-talk in the morning, with something like a cup of coffee (or other beverage), and then doing the same at night as part of your bedtime routine, the combined effect is extra powerful. Bookending your day with self-talk ingrains it deeply into your daily routine, in a way that's very easy to be consistent, because you never forget to drink your morning coffee, and you definitely never forget to go to bed.

Note: You don't need to have read Coffee Self-Talk prior to reading this book, but if you haven't read it, I highly recommend it because it's a life-changing morning ritual.

Pillow Self-Talk and Coffee Self-Talk both work on the same principles, but as we'll see, they differ in style and substance. And in their effects.

Are both forms of self-talk required for creating your magical life? No. You can do one or the other. *Or you can do what I do, which is both.* I infuse my entire day with as much positivity and elevated thoughts and feelings as I can, because it feels so friggin' good. I am my happiest when I do this. I feel my lightest and most joyful in my soul when I have my brain and heart aligned with good thoughts and feelings. It's what keeps me driven, focused, and attracting massive love and abundance. So, yeah. I do both, and I recommend you do too, if you want to maximize the magical vibes and fantastic results.

As you read through this book, and as you do your Pillow Self-Talk, you'll learn why the night has its own magical powers when it comes to self-talk, and how to use this special time to propel you faster toward your legendary life, like a rocket ship into the star-filled night sky. That's what you hold in your hands right now—a super-easy process you can start *tonight,* to live a better and happier life, to attract amazing things, people, and experiences to you, and to find more bliss, calm, and relaxation.

With this book, you'll learn about the massive importance of self-talk, and why it changes your life. You'll learn how to do the perfect bedtime routine to prepare for sleep, to feel good and chill out, and to slip effortlessly into peaceful relaxation as you drift off into dreamland.

There are a variety of special self-talk topics covered in this book, including:

- Star Bright Self-Love
- Astronomical Abundance
- Dazzling Relationships
- Magical Living & Spirituality
- Luminous Health, Healing & Longevity
- Celestial Surrender & Peace
- Eternal Happiness

Each of these sections includes pre-written scripts for specific goals and dreams you might seek, from discovering your own precious beauty and worth... to making money... to getting into the best shape of your life... to having the most incredible relationships... to addressing anxiety, stress, and grief.

So prop up your pillow, and slide between the comfy sheets of your bed. Tuck yourself in, and take a nice, long breath. *Let's get started!*

Sweetest dreams to you,

Kristen Helmstetter

PS. If you would like a free PDF with three bonus scripts not contained in this book, email me at:

Kristen@KristenHelmstetter.com

Be sure to mention that you want the "*Pillow Self-Talk Goodies.*"

PART I

CREATING YOUR DREAM LIFE WITH A SIMPLE NIGHTTIME RITUAL

Note: Instructions for how to do the 5-minute Pillow Self-Talk ritual are in Chapter 5. Actual Pillow Self-Talk scripts are in Part II of this book.

CHAPTER 1

WHAT IS SELF-TALK?

If the day and night be such that you greet them with joy, and life emits a fragrance like flowers and sweet-scented herbs... that is your success.

— HENRY DAVID THOREAU

In case you're new to self-talk, the next few pages will teach you all about it. If you've read *Coffee Self-Talk,* where I dive deeper into the topic, this is still a good refresher, so read on. (If you prefer to jump to the benefits of Pillow Self-Talk, skip to Chapter 2.)

"Self-talk" is simply the things you say to yourself, the things you think about yourself, the feelings and thoughts zipping through your mind about yourself, your life, and the world. It's what you say and think when you look at yourself in the mirror, or when you make a mistake, or when you celebrate a win. It's the way you talk to yourself.

That's it. Your thoughts and words to yourself. Your inner dialog.

So simple.

But so important!

We all use self-talk, whether we're aware of it or not. The key is that *how* we do our self-talk makes all the difference in how our lives unfold. Our self-talk makes the difference between living a life of bliss or crap, joy or despair, dreams or nightmares. This ongoing commentary in your head determines your focus, it determines your emotional state, and it's the most important part of whether you live an epic life. Or not.

And you have the power to control all of this. Simply by changing your self-talk.

I Made My Dreams Come True, and You Can, Too

I use positive self-talk every day. It puts me in a shimmering mood. I'd swear I sparkle like I just rolled in glue and crushed diamonds... but without the pain of getting poked all over, haha. But seriously, self-talk makes my life feel uplifted, like fresh air is flowing through me. It protects me, like a shiny, pink bulletproof vest. It keeps me perky, happy, and chill.

But that's not all...

My self-talk helps me manifest my *dreams and goals*. I use self-talk to attract prosperity, abundance, and money into my life. Ideas and opportunities come to me *all the time*. Literally, every day. I now fill journal after journal with ideas and notes... more than I'll ever need in a lifetime, and they just keep coming. Effortlessly. This did not always happen. It began when I started using self-talk for creativity and problem solving, and now I come up with all kinds of ideas for projects, product lines, and even entire businesses.

I use self-talk to help me stay healthy, too, by boosting my immune system and reducing stress. I've increased my courage. I've become more confident. And, as I described in *Coffee Self-Talk*, I even used these techniques to turn myself into a romance novelist. In my previous life, I never imagined I could write a single word of fiction, but I used a few, simple lines of self-talk to write *nine novels* in one year!

It was like magic.

In other words, there isn't a single part of my life where I don't use self-talk to make it remarkable... to make it *sparkle*. I've created a powerful, permanent state of mind.

Best of all, it was so easy! I want to shout it from the rooftops, because I've turned my life around, and anyone can do it. Anyone can be truly happy. Truly fulfilled. I changed the programming in my brain, simply by changing the things I say to myself, every day, day after day. And...

YOU CAN, TOO!

(That's me shouting to you from a rooftop. Did you hear it?)

Self-talk works because you're telling your brain what you want, and your brain takes the marching orders, no questions asked. It's like you made a blueprint for your brain, and it goes to work. Your life starts to change, based on that blueprint. Inspiration stirs within you, amazing synchronicities start to pop up everywhere, and you start to think, feel, and act differently, working to make your dreams and goals come true.

You're aware of part of it, because you're excited and motivated all the time, making plans, and taking action. It's *thrilling*, actually! But the real work—the heavy lifting of changing your attitudes, beliefs, and habitual behaviors—that all happens behind the scenes by your subconscious mind, without any effort on your part. It therefore feels a bit like a miracle. Like, good things just start to happen.

I started to notice a difference within just a few days.

When I went through this transformation, what's extra awesome is that it wasn't just me who was affected. My family has benefited *tremendously* from my perpetual happiness. I mean... who would you rather live with, right? Unhappy me or happy me?

(Happy me is definitely more fun!)

My ten-year-old daughter has witnessed me doing my self-talk, and now she's doing her own, too. I can actually see her self-esteem growing, and it nearly brings tears to my eyes. She sees me attracting my goals and manifesting my dreams with shooting-star speed, and it inspires her to set her own goals and watch the magic happen in her own life.

I am living proof of how *incredible* self-talk can change a life. And now, in this book, you're going to learn about one of my other self-talk rituals, my evening ritual: *Pillow Self-Talk.*

Why Self-Talk Is Vital to Your Well-Being

When you go about your daily life, you usually have a running commentary detailing life inside your brain. That little voice makes constant judgments and micro-decisions. It encourages you, and it cautions you. It can be your biggest helper. It can also be your greatest hindrance.

Do you believe you're a really great person? Do you consider yourself smart? Do you think you're weak? What about how you look... are you beautiful? What did you think of how your clothes fit today? How's your mood these days? Are you anxious? Courageous? Fearful? That's all self-talk.

As you can see, self-talk can be good or bad. In fact, every opinion and thought in your mind is influenced by your self-talk, and you can use this to your advantage to live your best life ever. You already possess this superpower, you just need to learn how to control it.

You can use your superpower to succeed beyond your wildest dreams. You can tap into it to accomplish things you never thought were possible. Do you have a desire to change your whole outlook on life? Do you want to fall asleep feeling safe, secure, and relaxed? Do you want to become healthier, calmer, lose weight, learn more, make more money, or have better relationships? Do you have a deep-rooted dream you long to pursue?

Your self-talk will help you do all of these things.

Here are some examples of positive self-talk:

I am beautiful, inside and out.

I am filled with peace tonight, and I fall asleep easily.

I have great time-management habits.

I'm living the luxury dream life of my design.

My self-worth is powerful. It opens doors of opportunities for me.

You choose the words, say them to yourself repeatedly, every day, and your brain just makes it happen.

It's straightforward cause-and-effect. You tell your brain what to do, and it goes to work, changing your thoughts, beliefs, and actions. Thousands of little decisions and actions, every day, mostly tiny things you aren't even aware of. These subconscious actions accumulate, leading you down a different path, changing you, and changing your entire life.

Best of all... it happens *fast.*

Bad habits and negative perspectives that you've held for *years* can sometimes be dissolved in days or a few weeks. The more often you repeat your self-talk, the faster the change happens. Frequency and consistency are a core part of the recipe. Which is why it's so important to complement your morning routine with a bedtime routine. That's twice as much self-talk!

Your subconscious believes whatever you tell it. If you tell yourself you're amazing, your brain gets to work making amazing things happen. You start to smile more. You start to feel amazing. You start seeing amazing opportunities. However, if you tell yourself you're always stressed out, then your brain looks for things to stress you out. If you always say you get sick every flu season, well, guess what? You're more likely to get sick.

This isn't voodoo, it's just the way our brains work.

Fortunately, it's brilliant in that we can create our most extraordinary lives by using positive self-talk. You give your beautiful brain the blueprint, the instructions, the directions, and it follows your orders like a good soldier. It's that simple.

Every single thing you think about yourself has an effect on your life. Every thought. Good or bad. Which is why there is *no room* in your magical, epic, legendary life for negative self-talk. So wrap all that crap up in a little box, thank it for its efforts, and send it on its way.

If you want the best life, then choose the best words. These "best" words will create the best thoughts, which will spin the best feelings in you, because the words you think and say about yourself *will create that life for you.* And you have the power to choose that life, right in your very own brain and mouth. *You! You! You!* (That's me shaking your shoulders with love, for effect.)

And when you have these amazing thoughts, there is a corresponding feeling that occurs, and it makes you feel good. Oh, it feels *really* good. And this combination of thinking and feeling is the key to manifesting your dreams. So get ready.

So... Is It Weird Being So Happy All the Time?

It is, kinda, at first.

Being so happy all the time, or responding to things with a playful shrug that other people would be freaking out about, giving me odd looks... yeah, it's weird. And bizarre. *And awesome!* Man, if only everyone did this. The world would be a much happier place.

Imagine the following:

"Oh, I'm so sorry I dented your car!"

"No problem! It looks better this way, anyway! I like the crunchy, new angles of the metal. Thank you!"

Kiss kiss, hug hug.

Ok, I'm kidding, a little, but I'm also serious. Happy vibes start with us. You, the reader. And me. And then watch what happens when enough of us do it at the same time. It's catchy, this happiness thing, and others will be like, *"What is she on? Give me some of that!"*

So, even if it feels weird. Do it.

Even if you don't believe your positive self-talk at first. Do it anyway.

You can start with the simplest phrase, like:

I am kind.

You can say this in the middle of a crap storm, and watch your soul relax a little.

That's part of the magic of self-talk. You don't even have to believe it at first, because your brain just fires and wires, without knowing the difference between what you are imagining and what is *really* happening. You can think of it as "rehearsing for success." And remember, pretty soon, you won't be pretending. You'll be living a brand-new reality. That you created. All with your brain.

Your Power. Your Choice. Your Responsibility.

I understand that we're all at different parts on our journey. There was a time in my life when my self-talk wasn't very good. But everything is different now. *Everything!* I live this life, and I work these principles every day. Now and forever.

It's your decision and nobody else's. It does not matter what anybody else does in your life. Not your mother or father, not your kids, not your partner, not your coworkers, or the angry person who honked at you or flipped you off. Not the news you hear on TV. Not social media. Your reaction, and your words, and your thoughts are *completely up to you.*

If you take responsibility for this basic truth, you will live the most amazing life ever.

Do you want to live a happier life? This is the way.

No matter what your childhood was like, no matter how abusive a relationship might have been, no matter how many cookies have crumbled around you... YOU are the one with the power to react any way you want.

And I can say all this with authority because I've been there. I've fallen, crashed, and been through my own traumas in life. But I dusted myself off and got back up. I stood tall and took control of my life.

It's the best thing I've ever done. Self-talk is the tool.

This Stuff Works!

Am I being repetitive? YES! I want this to *sink in*, so you won't be able to stop thinking about it! Excited! Telling your friends about this great, new, life-changing thing you've discovered. I will go on and on about how much better your life will be with your good self-talk, because it works. And remember, when it starts to work... *it will feel like magic.*

CHAPTER 2

WHAT IS PILLOW SELF-TALK?

When the world is draped in the mantle of night, the mirror of the mind is like the sky, in which thoughts twinkle like stars.

— KHUSHWANT SINGH

In the previous chapter, I explained the basics of self-talk. Now, I'll explain a special version of it that I call *Pillow Self-Talk.*

Pillow Self-Talk is a wonderful, super-cool bedtime ritual that will inspire you and relax the heck out of you, while simultaneously helping you manifest your goals and start living the life of your dreams.

While you sleep!

Pillow Self-Talk transforms your evening by preparing you to get your best sleep ever, and it helps you wake up feeling refreshed and excited to greet the day. This easy, five-minute bedtime ritual is incredibly powerful because it creates feelings of wholeness, worthiness, and self-love, and this is the foundation for creating your dream life. It also inspires creativity, whether you want to come up with clever ideas at work, or write, or paint, or invent something, or start a side business. And most of all, creativity helps you attract and create the life you've always dreamed of living.

Habit Stacking: The Brilliance of Pillow Self-Talk

One of the reasons my morning *Coffee Self-Talk* ritual is so easy is that it's an example of *habit stacking*. That is, it's taking something you do regularly—in this case, drinking coffee—and adding onto it something that you would like to start doing regularly. The coffee becomes a cue, or trigger, for doing the new behavior, and linking the two helps ensure that the new behavior becomes a permanent habit.

The first time I did Coffee Self-Talk, my mood changed *instantly*. I felt lighter. Happier.

And then I repeated it the next day, and the next... and in a few days, I was feeling lighter and happier *all the time*. Not just while having my coffee, but throughout the day.

My brain was *changing*.

As I continued doing this morning ritual, over the coming weeks, my whole life started to change. My mood, my energy level, my productivity, even my relationships... my family could see the difference!

With this idea of linking habits in mind, Pillow Self-Talk works the same way. Just as we're already drinking coffee every morning (or tea, or whatever), we're also already going to bed every night. But when many of us close our eyes at night, our thoughts are full of things that don't make us feel uplifted and happy.

At bedtime, many people's minds wander endlessly. About anxieties, or frustrations, or trivial things, like what they're going to eat for breakfast the next day, or what they did that day (or maybe what they didn't get done). Stuff that is, not only *not* useful, but can be harmful if you ruminate on things that stress you out, or keep you from falling asleep, or diminish the quality of your sleep.

So make a new ritual. A powerful, uplifting ritual! Where you say (or think) a few lines of positive self-talk during those minutes just before you fall asleep. Those few minutes have special meaning to your brain... they set the tone for the entire night.

Change what you say before bed, and your life will never be the same.

So, here it is: Pillow Self-Talk is taking five minutes before your head touches your pillow, and using your empowering self-talk in a special way to create life-changing benefits. Self-talk, in general, is extremely useful, but creating a special nighttime ritual with your self-talk fast-tracks your success and happiness, with a calm, relaxed mindset and an incredible night's sleep.

There's something magical about Pillow Self-Talk. It's the timing. It's the time just before you sleep, and you harness the power of self-talk to create feelings of relaxation and help you draw your dreams and goals to you faster.

It's gentle and calming, but don't let that fool you into thinking it's not as powerful as daytime self-talk, because it is. No matter what is going on in your life right now, Pillow Self-Talk can make it all feel much better.

Napoleon Hill said, *"Your subconscious mind works continuously, while you are awake, and while you sleep."* You get to take advantage of this phenomenon at bedtime by directing your subconscious to unlock connections, forge links you didn't know about, and find solutions to draw your dreams closer to you. So that's your task. That's your goal every night during the five minutes before you fall asleep.

You get to create the outcomes you seek.

You get to design your destiny, and your reality.

Before I started doing Pillow Self-Talk, I used to go to bed with my mind running wild about the day I'd just completed, overly excited for the next one to come. It was mostly good stuff, but I was restless with the excitement and planning. My mind was *go-go-go*. I had so many opportunities coming to me, so many ideas, which is all fabulous, right? But it kept my mind in beta brainwaves, analyzing and planning, when I should've been in alpha, for relaxation, before going to sleep.

Visualizations and suggestions—that is, your dreams and goals, and your self-talk—will be most readily accepted by your subconscious mind when you are deeply relaxed. This makes doing self-talk just before sleep perfect timing. As you'll see, I'm going to show you a special type of self-talk for this special time of day: affirmations— spoken like a mantra—that have a calming, almost hypnotic effect.

The ritual involves using self-talk with scripts, *and a special method*, before bedtime. I've filled this book with sections covering different areas of your life that you might want to address, such as:

- Self-love
- Prosperity & abundance
- Money & investing
- Confidence
- Creativity
- Love & intimacy
- Parenting
- Friendships
- Magical living
- Spirituality
- Health & fitness
- Energy
- Happiness
- Stress & anxiety
- Letting go & calmness

You'll choose just one topic each night. Each section includes a pre-written script of positive self-talk for you to read, along with a special mantra to say as you fall asleep. We'll go into the details later. For now, just get excited, knowing that you can work on any aspect of your life during this special, relaxed nighttime ritual.

I mentioned Coffee Self-Talk in the introduction. Here's how Pillow Self-Talk differs: You see, Coffee Self-Talk helps you live your most magical life by helping you accomplish your goals with joy, gusto, awe, and pizazz. But it does so in a way that *amps you up*, and you feel empowered, sizzling, dazzling, magnetic, thrilled. And most of all, *worthy*. Worthy to receive, worthy to live the life of your dreams, and become the person you dream of being. With Coffee Self-Talk, elevated emotions of mind-blowing excitement swirl through you. It's incredibly effective.

Pillow Self-Talk is different. Because it's bedtime, instead of getting fired up, you want to take advantage of this unique time of day to focus on creating a relaxed, chill, and calm state of mind. You're not donning your superhero cape here. You're grabbing your sleep mask, if you like. Or hugging your teddy bear.

That's not to say you can't feel chill and relaxed with Coffee Self-Talk, because you can, if that's your focus. It's just that many people choose to pump themselves up during their morning ritual. Which is not the elevated emotion we want before going to bed. With Pillow Self-Talk, you don't go to lie down with your brain all lit up and excited, because you'd never fall asleep.

Pillow Self-Talk is designed to take advantage of the power of elevated emotions for making your dreams come true, but by guiding you through the equally influential feelings of *relaxation, peace, and calm*. These specific feelings help you live your best life and accomplish your goals in a similar way to the elevated feelings of love, awe, excitement, and joy, but they're on the other end of the energy spectrum.

Later, I'll explain why elevated emotions are critical for manifesting your dreams. But for now, suffice it to say, you want good feelings and happy emotions to accompany your Pillow Self-Talk ritual, not stress or anxiety. We have a lot of elevated emotions to choose from, and some of them are fantastic for giving you an amazing night's sleep.

You effortlessly tap into peaceful, calm feelings, with your shoulders relaxed. Stress is diminished, and troubling anxiety is reduced. Or eliminated altogether. You infuse yourself with bliss, worthiness, love, and the most profound tranquility imaginable. With Pillow Self-Talk, you find peace and get the best sleep, and all of these support your dream life coming straight to you.

This entire process is vital because your thoughts and feelings at any given time determine your focus. And your focus determines your reality. It drives your life... literally, determining which direction you go, and where you end up. So, by having calm, chilled-out, relaxed feelings, with specially designed self-talk, you guide yourself straight toward living the life of your dreams.

CHAPTER 3

THE BENEFITS OF PILLOW SELF-TALK

The things of the night cannot be explained in the day, because they do not then exist.

— ERNEST HEMINGWAY

I've touched briefly on some of the benefits of Pillow Self-Talk. In this chapter, I'll explore the five main benefits in detail.

Benefit #1: Peace of Mind, Now

One of the most striking benefits of Pillow Self-Talk is the immediate feeling of relaxation as you get ready for bed. Pillow Self-Talk makes you feel calm from the moment you start doing it. As you read the words and feel the corresponding feelings that go along with those words, your heart and mind begin to expand. You start to imagine possibilities, and you're totally chilled out.

Your increased peace and relaxation gives you a great sleep, and this helps you address negative thought patterns and emotions from a long day. And as you sleep, your peaceful mindset boosts your creativity. You might even find yourself finding solutions to real-world problems in your beautiful, vivid dreams.

Over time, as your self-talk transforms you into a new person, with a great attitude and sparkling new thoughts and feelings... you create a new life. One filled with abundance, health, energy, prosperity, and love.

I often talk about how amazing self-talk is when it's amping up life, making you excited and energized, but the flip side to this is the peaceful happiness you experience, because you can drastically reduce feelings of stress. Your Pillow Self-Talk will decrease low-vibe, survival emotions like anxiety and fear.

When you focus your attention on what's going on inside of you, finding the good, then you won't be dependent on what's happening outside of you to make you happy.

This gives you power! It gives you *control over your life.*

Benefit #2: The Self-Love Transformation

Self-love is, without a doubt, the most important benefit of positive self-talk. I'm listing it here as number two because the first benefit, peace of mind, can happen right away. And, yes, for some people, loving yourself will happen right away as well. But some people will take more time to love themselves. Either way, it will happen with this Pillow Self-Talk ritual if you keep it up every night.

You see, manifesting your dreams ultimately comes down to self-love. It's a necessary precondition. Without self-love, you may not feel worthy to receive the life of your dreams, and your subconscious will sabotage the process. When you love yourself, only then can your heart and emotions be aligned with your conscious desires... your goals. And your self-talk is the best way to get there, building up your sense of self-worth and self-love so intensely that your heart and mind are in total sync with reaching your dreams.

What else happens when you love yourself? You *enjoy* the person you are. Your self-esteem shines. You become your own best friend, your greatest ally, your biggest cheerleader, and these combine to make the most brilliant life, no matter what is going on in the world around you.

Why does this matter?

When you love yourself, everything around you changes. Your confidence is dramatically boosted, and when that happens, you put yourself out into the world more, and more opportunities come to you as a result. When you love yourself, your energy becomes magnetic, and more people want to be around you. This gives you more opportunities for success with your career, relationships, abundance, and people's general willingness to be friendly and help you. This help comes in a thousand tiny ways, and occasionally in big ways. Sometimes even in life-changing ways. All because of the happy, radiant energy that you give off.

Loving yourself gives you a relaxed courage and drive to make better choices. To take chances. To think more creatively. You'll find yourself thinking outside-the-box in all kinds of situations in life, both personal and professional. You won't be moved by the negative opinions of others. You'll also lose the need to judge others, or compare others to yourself. Instead, you'll feel compassion. And loving yourself gives you permission to be calm in any storm. Just imagine, riding through life's ups and downs, with a smile on your face and song in your heart. That's self-love.

As each night passes, you'll fall more in love with yourself, making your dreams easier to attain, because you *really do* start to believe in yourself. And that's when everything else in your life will start to click, as though the universe suddenly started pulling strings to make it happen. Don't underestimate the power your self-love has for making your dreams come true and attaining your goals.

Here's the rule to live by:

Loving yourself is a prerequisite to manifesting your dreams.

The self-love affirmations in the scripts in Part II of this book are designed very specifically to program your brain with self-love and self-belief. Once you've programmed your brain to believe, *and feel*, thoughts such as these, they will become internalized and manifest in all kinds of wonderful ways, some of which will be apparent to the outside world, and many of which will exist in your own internal, blissful, happy, magical state-of-mind.

One thing is for sure. You'll never go back to the life you were living, before you started your self-talk, and before you started fully loving yourself.

Benefit #3: Your Best Sleep Ever for Your Most Magical Life

One of the easiest, no-brainer benefits of Pillow Self-Talk is that it helps you get the best damn sleep *ever*.

Sleep is a magical elixir for living a brilliant life, and it's right there, ready to take advantage of, eager to support all of your dreams and goals... *if* you get enough good sleep each night.

How does sleep help manifest your dreams?

With quality sleep, you show up to your life each day, ready to rock-n-roll. You have more energy. More mental clarity. You're more rested and relaxed. You're calmer. And you put out an elevated vibe, which helps directly with manifesting your dreams and goals. Getting good sleep is like greasing the track on your train of joy. Your mindset is open, and you're recharged and ready for your next day, sparkling bright.

You know that sleep is important. You hear it all the time. Yet many people don't do anything about it. They don't make it a priority. According to the CDC, one in three adults doesn't get enough sleep. And according to sleep expert Matthew Walker, the estimated annual lost income from sleep deprivation in the U.S. is about $411 billion.

Are you one of those people? Maybe you didn't take your sleep seriously before now, but that was before you knew that quality sleep was so instrumental to living your magical life and helping you make your dreams come true. It can help you manifest creativity, prosperity, love, romance, success, abundance, and a happy mindset. Now you might take a second look at prioritizing sleep and your evening routine to improve your sleep quality.

And guess what?

Pillow Self-Talk is going to help you get the quality of sleep you deserve.

As with any goal, stating your "compelling *why*" is important for ensuring that you follow through. I've already stated a few reasons why getting good sleep is important, but I'm going to lay a few more facts on you, just for good measure...

For starters, really cool health improvements happen with good sleep.

Things like a stronger immune system and better hormone function, plus helping with healing and recovery, preserving your DNA, and even helping you manage your ideal bodyweight. I could go on and on.

And your mood! Holy smokes!... Getting enough sleep is one of *the best* ways to lift your mood. According to Matthew Walker,

> "*A study of over twenty thousand people found that falling just one hour short of the optimum amount of sleep—seven to nine hours—was associated with a 60 to 80 percent increased risk of experiencing negative moods, like hopelessness and nervousness.*"

That is *not* living a legendary life!

But with a lovely night's sleep? Your patience is increased, and the rough edges of life are smoothed, because your emotions are soothed. Quality sleep actually helps you process strenuous emotional memories—*how neat is that?* Dr. Christiane Northrup writes in her book, *Goddesses Never Age*, "*Sleep is, hands down, the most effective way to metabolize excess stress hormones.*" So if you have an emotional day, by making sleep your priority, you can have your brain work on solving your troubles while you get your zzz's.

Learning and memory are improved, even motor skills... *while you sleep!*

Get this... Matthew Walker says that the brain enhances the motor skills of something you have previously practiced, while you sleep. In other words, after your practice, and after a good sleep, when you come back the next day, your motor skills performance can be 20–30% better than where you left off the day before. *Whaaaat?*

How fascinating, that our brains continue to learn—without further practice—hours after the training session.

Good quality sleep optimizes you for peak performance, and it helps you harness your creative genius.

Did you know that problem-solving and creativity can come to you in your dreams? Get this:

- Einstein conceived his theory of Special Relativity while sleeping on a train. You know... $E = mc^2$? Yeah, that one.
- Dmitri Mendeleev created the Periodic Table of the Elements... in his sleep. Whoa!
- Paul McCartney's song, *Let It Be,* came to him in a dream.
- But here's my fave... Elias Howe was freaking out because he was in debt up to his arse trying to invent a machine that could stitch cloth, but none of his ideas had worked. One night, he dreamt that his creditors were surrounding him, about to skewer him with spears. He looked down and saw...

wait for it... *holes in the spear tips.* He awoke in a flash, realizing that the hole needed to go *in the front of the needle,* not the back! And that's how he invented the sewing machine.

This comes from the book, *Where Good Ideas Come From,*

"We conventionally associate dream inspiration with the creative arts, but the canon of scientific breakthroughs contain many revolutionary ideas that originated in dreams."

I, myself, have come up with story ideas in my dreams. So has my husband. His young readers book, *Mystery of the Haunted Cider Mill,* came to him fully formed in a dream, down to the tiniest details.

So, if you're a creative, then you absolutely *must* prioritize sleep. But even if you don't consider yourself "a creative," realize that *all activities in life* benefit from having access to your brain's ability to generate alternate solutions. Creativity isn't something that's reserved just for painters and writers... it's the ability to make new connections, or new ideas to try out, and that can help anybody! Creativity could be a different route to drive to work, or something that makes your job easier, which could lead to a raise or a promotion. It's a superpower that's available to all humans. *Everybody.*

And sleep taps into that magic juju!

Ok. Let's recap. Good sleep is one of your new top priorities because good sleep helps you feel better and think better, and *that* helps you manifest your best life!

In other words, sleep is really freakin' important to living your magical life.

There's no way around that.

And that's where your Pillow Self-Talk comes in. Be excited, because, if getting good sleep has been a challenge for you, it's going to get better. Your Pillow Self-Talk will help you wind down after your day. It'll help put you in a good mood, so you fall into blissful sleep, relaxed, with a soft smile on your face.

Most importantly, it will prime your heart and soul for your magical dreamland.

Benefit #4: Memory Consolidation and the Tetris Effect... Here's Where Things Get Weird

Here comes the grooviest part... Pillow Self-Talk is particularly beneficial at bedtime because it's a very special time for the brain. You're about to enter an eight-hour block of time, during which your subconsciousness is in charge. This is the perfect opportunity to *prime* your brain with self-talk, almost like hypnosis.

You see, choosing carefully what you think about immediately before you go to sleep is one of the most important things you can do to change your life. I'll say that again: What you *think about*, what you're *saying to yourself*, what words and ideas are running through your mind can determine *how* you sleep, and that determines how you *feel*. These queue up the night's agenda for your subconscious mind to process.

And what does the subconscious do while we sleep?

Nobody knows... *it's magic.*

Well, not really. We know a little. We know that the brain consolidates the day's short-term memories into long-term memory. Or put another way, we *learn*. This is literally when the brain does its permanent wiring. In fact, studies have shown that students who study right before bed learn the material better, and it's likely due to this memory consolidation. This might even be one of the main reasons we sleep!

Think about that, studying before bed... self-talk is no different. Say your self-talk before bed, and it gets wired straight into your long-term memory that very night.

That is, it becomes *permanent.*

How exciting!

It's especially exciting when you realize that speaking your words *with emotion*—I mean, really feeling it, deep down in your soul—sends an urgent message to your brain that says, *This is important, be sure to remember it permanently while I'm sleeping tonight.*

So, Pillow Self-Talk is utilizing three memory hacks simultaneously. Each of them is known to impact learning and memory. Taken together, they pack an *extra* powerful punch when it comes to rewiring your brain for living your epic dream life. The three hacks are:

- Saying the words last thing before you go to sleep
- Adding emotion to the words you say, and really feeling it
- Repetition, because you're doing this night after night

Your brain can't help but get the message, loud and clear, that

THIS STUFF IS IMPORTANT. MAKE IT HAPPEN!

The Tetris Effect

There's an interesting phenomenon called *The Tetris Effect,* based on the classic block-stacking video game, *Tetris.* People who play the game before bed often report seeing the stacking blocks when they close their eyes before going to sleep. This also happens with other sensory experiences, such as sounds and motion.

There's a transitional period between wakefulness and sleep known as the *hypnagogic* state of consciousness. We've all experienced it... it's that time when you're drifting off to sleep, and you sometimes have weird mini-dreams. Dr. Sara Mednick (Department of Psychology, University of California, Riverside) describes hypnagogic sleep as a state in which "the mind is fluid and hyper-associative," meaning it brings together unusual ideas in novel ways. In other words, *mega creativity*. For this reason, for centuries, brilliant people—including Isaac Newton, Thomas Edison, Nikola Tesla, Beethoven, and Salvador Dalí—have taken advantage of this transitional period to beef up their creative brilliance.

During this hypnagogic state, you're particularly open to suggestion, much like during hypnosis. For the same reason your brain accepts wildly outlandish hypnagogic dreams—which seem absurd or confusing if you happen to wake up and remember them—when you're in the hypnagogic state, it similarly accepts self-talk affirmations that are not yet true, but that you are working toward.

Pillow self-talk takes advantage of the Tetris affect, combined with the hypnagogic state. That is, when you repeat your self-talk just before you go to sleep, it's not only fresh in your memory, but it can also replay itself in a kind of automated loop as you drift off to sleep, especially if it's the last thing you hear before slipping into the transitional, half-awake-half-asleep hypnagogic state.

It's kind of an awesome brain hack... programming your brain with the most powerful, uplifting, amazing words... at the exact moment that your mind does a handoff from conscious to subconscious control. Those sweet words get loaded straight into the night's memory consolidation program. They might even make an appearance in your dreams!

It's a powerful way to imprint anything you want into your subconscious, which causes you to look for, or notice, related things during the day, when you're awake.

This is important because, if you fall asleep thinking and feeling about the future you're drawing to you, as if you're living it now, and you flood your mind with these words, thoughts, images, and emotions as you drift asleep, then you wake up the following day with your eyes wide open for opportunities, success, creativity, or any number of things that will bring your dream closer to reality. You've primed your brain to see things you otherwise might not have noticed, and this is one of the reasons manifesting your dreams can result directly from doing your Pillow Self-Talk every night. When you have such a strong, laser-like focus on whatever it is that you want, you tend to see more opportunities to get it, or you come up with ideas for attracting and attaining it.

As Thomas Edison said,

"Never go to sleep without a request to your subconscious."

This quote always amazes me... he knew a hundred years ago what modern neuroscience is proving: At bedtime, we have the power to literally *direct* our subconscious mind to work on our requests, dreams, and creative breakthroughs... *while we sleep.*

Prior to sleep, I focus on a specific direction to my powerful subconscious mind with a line from my Pillow Self-Talk, and then *it goes to work for me,* helping make my dreams a reality.

I get into a nice, sleepy state, and I focus my mind, by affirming slowly and with calm feelings, *one specific* statement of my self-talk. This is the *Pillow Self-Talk Mantra* (which I explain in Chapter 5). I repeat it quietly and lovingly as I fall into deep and dreamy, healing, restful sleep. Each time I repeat the words, the emotional value intensifies, and I feel a kind of *knowing* start to seep into my soul. It feels so good falling asleep this way, like I'm gently rocking my subconscious to sleep. (I'll teach you exactly how to do this later.)

And what are my results?

Well, I liken it to the people who play Tetris repeatedly over several days, when they start "seeing" how different shapes *in the real world* can fit together. For example, they might look in their pantry and start imaging different ways to organize boxes of food, or they might be walking in a city and start imagining the buildings stacking together. Groovy, huh?... I mean, ok, it's a little scary when a freakin' video game takes over your brain... but when it's my own, deliberate self-talk?... Sign my ass up for that neuro magic!

It really works. My nighttime routine has trained my daytime brain to see things differently. Now, when I go through the daytime part of my day, my brain notices *all kinds of things* that are helpful to manifesting my dream life. I see patterns I never saw before. I see possibilities. I see opportunities. My creative juices flow for writing books and building my business. All because of my relaxed and repeated focus as I fall asleep each night.

Benefit #5: Radical Resilience

Resilience refers to a person's ability to bounce back after experiencing a setback. Pillow Self-Talk brings with it radical resilience for your life in many ways.

Part of the resilience is simply because it helps you get a great sleep, which makes you more robust physically.

It creates emotional resilience, too, though. You can use your self-talk at night to secure your emotions and keep them running smooth. With your emotions relaxed and in-check, you find yourself going with the flow in life. Things don't rile you up anymore.

Doing Pillow Self-Talk before bed helps you process the day. If you had a busy or hectic day, it'll help your mind relax so you don't obsess about it. If you had a particularly "off" day, then it's a beautiful way to help you find peace of mind. And this brings a night full of restful sleep, which builds resilience.

And, you see, this resilience breeds incredible courage. Imagine walking through your day with confidence. It empowers you, making you feel strong and alive, ready for anything. It makes you willing to try new things... the very things that are *necessary* to live the life of your dreams. It will no longer matter if fear taps you on your shoulder, because your courage and confidence will move your feet, taking steps in the direction of your goals.

How Are All These Wonderful Benefits Even Possible? Magicky Science Stuff.

I like to think it's all quite magical, these benefits, because it's just fun to think about it that way, and it sure feels like magic. I mean, when you can go from a foul mood to a bubbly mood, simply by shifting your thoughts, it makes you do a double take.

But it's not actually magic. It's science. That's because self-talk changes the structure of your brain, which makes it the best superpower in the galaxy. Human brains are *neuroplastic*, which means they can change, no matter what age you are. This is how we can learn new skills, like playing the piano or learning a new language. Our brains are super flexible, and you can constantly build new neural pathways. This is important. It's how self-talk can change your life.

Here's a neat example from ScienceFocus.com:

> *"Psychologists at the University of Sheffield in England tested this... They gave half of their volunteers the following instruction before the weekend, and asked them to repeat it three times, and to commit to doing it: 'If I am deciding what to do this weekend, then I will select activities that will make me feel good and avoid doing things that will make me feel bad!'*
>
> *"On Monday, ... those who followed the instruction experienced more positive emotion over the weekend. This was particularly the case for the volunteers with more neurotic personalities, who said they usually struggled to regulate their emotions."*

Amazing. You can just choose to do things that make you happy.

The trick is to do this repeatedly. The more you think positive thoughts, and the more you say positive things about yourself, the more your brain will fire and wire it that way. It's like walking on a path through the woods. The more you do it, the deeper the path gets, and as a result, it's easier to tap into elevated feelings and thoughts anytime you want. It becomes baked into your brain and your mindset, like an imprint on your soul.

Remember: When you change your thoughts, you change your focus. This changes your brain. And *this* changes your reality.

I usually wake up in a positive mood. Upon opening my eyes, if any shadow lurks on the outskirts of my mind, I say out loud as I swing my legs off my bed, *"Today, I'm going to have an amazing day."* The lurking thoughts shy away from me... they know not to mess with me.

Everything is easier with the way my brain is now. When life doesn't go the way I'd like, I just shrug. And then, *I actually get excited*, knowing and feeling that life is about to get even better.

I wasn't like this as a kid.

I wasn't like this as a young adult.

I trained my brain into this with *practice*.

And now, it's *effortless* to find joy.

As you reduce your negative self-talk, over time, negative thoughts feel more foreign to you. Those pathways in your brain don't get used. Those thoughts go into retirement, until they are no longer a part of your life.

New focus. New you.

New thinking. New you.

New behaviors. New you.

New amazing life!

And incredibly, this transformation can occur in just a few weeks, no matter your age or circumstances in your life right now.

The Secret Recipe to Manifestation: Thinking + Feeling with Visioneering

Using positive self-talk is going to make your life better. You understand that by now... you *get it*. But there is a way to fast-track this. A way to add rocket fuel to your trip to the stars.

Enter: Visioneering

Something magical happens when you combine the following four things:

1. Self-talk
2. Elevated emotions (love, awe, gratitude, etc.)
3. Closing your eyes and visualizing your future in ways you can actually see in your mind's eye (vivid mental pictures)
4. All while you're drifting off to sleep

I call this process *visioneering.*

Visioneering is my term for a special *Manifestation Recipe*. It means that I'm *engineering the vision* of my future life.

Basically, you imagine your future, like you're seeing a vision. Your mental vision could be like a photograph, or a movie, or even a dream. I usually do this with my eyes closed, which is why bedtime is great. And in this future vision of the *life that you're designing*, you feel amazing, because you manifested what you want in this vision. You imagine yourself as the person you dream of being: loving, worthy, successful, whole and healed, having peace of mind, creative, glowing, and shimmering.

Living the dream.

Your dream!

Then, you take the image, this person, *you*, that exists in your vision, and you take the life you're living *in your vision of the future*, and you place the picture over yourself, now, like a second skin. Like a flat sheet you snap up over your bed, and it falls down, draping gently over you and the mattress.

I know, it sounds weird... but it works. When I do this, I see my future self: I'm healthy, strong, free to choose my own schedule, I'm successful, a prolific writer, awesomely wealthy, living a life of abundance, surrounded by loving relationships. I'm calm, and bright, and full of energy. Sometimes, I'm standing in a forest near the mountains. Other times, I'm on the cliffs in Cabo, watching the sun set over the Pacific, with the wind from the ocean whipping through my hair.

Oh, and in my Cabo vision, I'm wearing a flowing, white dress and turquoise jewelry. See yourself in as much detail as you can!

When I drape that beautiful picture *over my body like a second skin*, I become a new me. I *feeeeeeel* how amazing all of those things being true about me would feel. My emotions flourish with elevated sensations, and in my mind, I become this new person, and my body responds with the emotions *as if it's true*.

There's a feeling of *expectancy*. More on that in a bit.

So think about that. Visioneering... engineering your vision of what you want: your worthiness, your abundance, your peace of mind, your wholeness and healing, your courage, your *bestest*, most awesome life. And you marry the elevated emotions to it. It's like a magnet for your dreams. When you add good feelings, you amplify the total experience tremendously.

For my visioneering, I get specific in the *what I am* and the *where I am*... I see these clearly in my mind. But the *how*? I don't focus on that. The how will happen naturally with all the opportunities I'll now start to see in my "waking" life and attract from this exercise.

This vibe you emit helps draw your goals to you. It can come in many forms. Maybe it's a job offer from out of the blue. Or a promotion. Maybe someone approaches you with a business idea—and the only reason they did was because they "had a good feeling about you." When you send out a positive vibe, people notice.

Other times, your energy may help you attract what you seek based on your increased creativity and ability to come up with good ideas and solve problems. Other times, the energy gives you the confidence to go boldly in the direction of your dreams, whether that means stretching beyond your comfort zone, taking risks, or simply reaching out for something you've deserved for a long time, but your internal resistance held you back. There are many ways your elevated energy helps you attract your best life. But all of them are driven by your positive feelings.

That's why the key to successful self-talk is to match up the thoughts with the feelings. It's not that difficult to do, because you automatically *will* start to feel those good feelings when you consistently think those good thoughts.

When you read the self-talk scripts later in this book, you want to say the words as if they're gospel. Act *as if*. Affirm it as your truth. And if it were true, how would you *act and feel* while reading them? You'd be totally chill because, remember, these scripts are designed to fit with winding down and relaxing as you prepare to sleep. Even if you're generally a high-energy person, this calm sensation is deeply satisfying... it suggests a kind of confidence, like you know everything is as it should be.

When you expect the best, you're chill with the rest.

There's magic in this.

The Power of Your Happy Expectation

Is it possible to be chill and excited at the same time?

Yes!

Welcome to the concept I call *Happy Expectation.*

Remember when you were a kid, and you wanted something for your birthday... and you knew you were going to get it? How did you feel from the time you found out you'd be getting it, to the time you actually received it? You were probably thrilled, but chilled. Excited about your new, fun gift, and also relaxed, because you knew it was coming.

Or when you knew you'd be getting a promotion, or a bonus, and it was only a matter of time. Or that time you were excited about taking a trip to Disney World or Paris, and you were also peaceful, because you knew it was coming.

This is the power of *Happy Expectation.* It's the feeling you have when excitement is combined with certainty about the thing happening.

It creates an excitement and a *knowing.* An expectation that it's all going to work out, and you'll get what you want. Because you're worthy, of course. And as a result, you're not stressed. This is a powerful feeling when it comes to manifesting. And that's what you want to tap into with your Pillow Self-Talk. You'll think about your goals and dreams... those are the fun, magical thoughts swirling in your head. But those thoughts will be dancing with the relaxed, Happy Expectation vibe coming from your heart. It's like they're dancing together to some groovy jazz tune, calm and confident.

All is well, and all good things are coming. Doesn't that sound good?

How Long Does It Take to Work?

From your very first Pillow Self-Talk session, you will notice the benefits, as it relaxes you, inspires you, and excites you, because you know you're making a major life change. The *anticipation* of this new ritual is of great value, and it feels good. You'll just read any script from Part II, adding your own lines that give you peace or spark joy. You'll do the simple process detailed in Chapter 5, and that's it. It starts the ball rolling in the right direction.

It really is that simple.

What About the Long-Term Benefits?

For lasting change, it's all about *repetition*. The more consistent you are, the faster the results will be. Which is why I recommend doing your Pillow Self-Talk every night.

And repetition is also why Pillow Self-Talk is just one of my daily self-talk rituals... I do my Coffee Self-Talk every morning, too. If I were only doing Pillow Self-Talk, then yes, of course, there are short and long-term benefits. But when I combine it with Coffee Self-Talk, I'm doubling the frequency, and this wires up my brain with Hulk-strength wires, which means I'll experience the benefits that much sooner.

The strength of the connections in your brain also depends on the level of feeling and elevated emotion you experience while doing your self-talk. Firing and wiring together are definitely driven by frequency, but the level of emotions you employ will have a huge impact, too.

So when you do your self-talk ritual repeatedly, the results come faster. Positive self-talk has a lot to do with optimism, and even if you need to fake it initially, that's totally fine, because it will start to feel real—and *be* real—the more you do it. You're essentially strengthening your optimism muscle... I call it my *happy muscle*. Your job is simply to show up and do the reps, like when you're in a gym doing bicep curls. That is, the good self-talk. And all of these wonderful thoughts and feelings just automatically get stronger and stronger over time, without any real effort on your part, other than saying the words, every night, ideally with emotion. Make this ritual a frequent habit, and that's exactly what *joy and happiness* will be... your *habit*. Your default. Your norm.

The new you.

Your Life Is Up to You

That's the plain truth of the matter. Your self-talk is either positive, or negative, or somewhere in-between. You get to choose. You are responsible for how you think. You are responsible for how you feel. You can't control everything, but you are in charge of 100% of your reactions. You are the master conductor of your life. That means no one else is.

So don't make excuses. Don't give yourself excuses. If you want this, then go for it. Take the time to do your self-talk, and Pillow Self-Talk is one of the easiest ways to start. If you're also doing your Coffee Self-Talk, then keep it up! I've heard from so many people, from all walks of life, from age five to 85, in all kinds of situations, and from all kinds of past experiences, making the most profound changes in their lives.

If they can do it, so can you.

Now you know the power *you have*. And with this knowledge comes the power of knowing that you are in charge of how you feel. That means YOU are in charge of what you attract into your life. All the greatness that life has to offer.

It's yours for the taking.

CHAPTER 4

THE POWER OF RITUAL AND ENVIRONMENT

I want night, deep ambrosial night.

— GEORG BÜCHNER

Before we jump into the steps for doing your Pillow Self-Talk (which will be in the next chapter), I want to explain the importance of performing your self-talk like a *ritual*. This is something special. Something bigger than brushing your teeth before bed. *Much* bigger.

When you make something a ritual, you give it a special meaning, and your brain perks up. It takes notice because there's a magical feeling that comes with that word. Maybe it stems from thinking of rituals as mystical, or religious, or sacred in some way, or perhaps from childhood stories with witches conjuring spells under a full moon. For whatever the reason, rituals bring a sense of the extraordinary, and they give special meaning to whatever you're doing in that moment. They're like mini-celebrations, and I love thinking of Pillow Self-Talk this way. Celebrating my life, with good thoughts and feelings that make my dreams come true. And that is something totally worth celebrating.

So that's how I view my Pillow Self-Talk, *a powerful ritual.* I feel the same way about my Coffee Self-Talk. And having these two rituals bookend my day has created a mind-blowing existence I never knew was possible.

Viewing Pillow Self-Talk as your evening ritual is also smart, because it'll make you want to do it every night. And there is power in having the proper environment to support that ritual, because you can make the whole experience more effective with specially chosen surroundings in your bedroom. The synergy of the ritual plus environment draws you in, like a moth to a light, and this encourages your new behavior. You look forward to it. In fact, after a short while, you crave it.

In Chapter 3, I discussed how important it is to have really good sleep, due to its ability to help you manifest your goals. With that in mind, let's focus on a couple of things you can do to improve the quality of your sleep, because, as it improves, you'll reap immense benefits on a physical, mental, and spiritual level.

Your #1 Sleep Goal: Stick to a Routine Sleep Schedule

Humans are creatures of habit. Our brains are wired such that, anything we do repeatedly becomes somewhat automated and efficient. There's absolutely a time for variety and novelty in your day... your bedtime routine is not one of them. The more you can standardize what you do for the half hour or so leading up to bed, the easier it will be to fall asleep.

Establishing a consistent sleep routine is probably the single most important thing you can do to get good sleep. That is, simply going to sleep every night and waking up at the same time every day. So, this is now an important part of your new *Pillow Self-Talk Ritual.* Inspect your schedule, and figure out what time you need (or want) to wake up every day, and work backward from there to figure out when to go to bed. Your goal is 7 to 9 hours of sleep each night.

Here's the critical part: Stick to this schedule *every day!* I repeat, a regular sleep routine is one of *the most effective ways* to get the excellent sleep *you deserve*. This includes the weekends. If you want the best sleep experience, if you want to support your most magical life, then get the best sleep possible.

That's the promise of a *consistent* sleep routine.

The best way to do this is to set a *bedtime* alarm. People set alarms to wake up... well, I set an alarm to start getting ready for bed. If I want to be *sleeping* at 10:00 PM every night, then at 9:00 PM, I have an entry in my phone's calendar labeled "Pillow Self-Talk," and that's when my bedtime ritual begins. I dim the lights, I don my blue-blocking glasses, I play certain music, and I slowly ease into a relaxed mood as I go about getting ready for bed.

Perfect Your Sleep Environment

The more amazing your environment for your Pillow Self-Talk, the more elevated emotional state you can easily tap into. The right environment makes it effortless. When you're intentional about your sleep environment, you can shape it to amplify your experience, your emotions, and your feelings. That's important for your Pillow Self-Talk time because it makes the *entire process* more intentional. It gives your nightly ritual a heavier weight and deeper meaning, which makes for a more profound experience.

You want to love the space you're in while you do your Pillow Self-Talk because it will boost your mood and keep you motivated to stick with your ritual every night.

So make it special. Optimize for the win.

Here are some ways to help you fine-tune your environment for getting the world's best sleep. As you decide what to do with your own private sanctuary—your bedroom—I want you to think about *your senses*. What can you do with sight, sound, touch, taste, and smell that you can reserve as special, to anchor to your Pillow Self-Talk and bedtime? Once you create these sense anchors, it's important to *only use them for this purpose* going forward, otherwise they will lose their power as anchors.

Light & Darkness

About an hour before bed, I start turning off the bright, overhead lights in my home, and use only small lamps when possible. I have a few of those realistic-looking LED candles to light the hallway. They cast a warm glow that's bright enough to see my way, but that's all.

As the ambient light level drops, this sends a signal to my brain that it's time to start winding things down. Remember, we're wired to be creatures of habit. If you're consistent with things like turning down the lights an hour before bed, just like Pavlov's dogs, your brain's natural response to the dimmer light will be to dial down your energy and start releasing hormones to make you feel tired.

You might want to put a gorgeous salt lamp in your bedroom that you only turn on once you're winding down to get ready for bed. Or have a pretty candle that you light for the evening. The warm, yellow-orange glow is not only beautiful, it also sets a kind of quiet, contemplative mood, which harkens back to the campfires of our ancient past.

And what's the exact opposite of this?

So-called "blue light," from TVs, phones, and computers. It's not actually blue, like the sky... it's called "blue" because of what's called the *color temperature* used in the white light on these devices. White with more blue in it is called a "cooler" white, and it has a bluish tint that's noticeable if you hold it up to a "warmer" white, which has a more yellowish tint.

And this blue light is *terrible* for your sleep!

Artificial blue light is basically sending a confusing signal to the part of the brain that controls your circadian rhythm, which means your daily sleep/wakefulness cycle. As you're probably aware, this cycle is hugely affected by light. Bright equals day, dark equals night. But it's also affected by the light's *color*. Blue-tinted light signals "daylight" to your brain, which in turn tries to keep you awake. It does so by disrupting your brain's efforts to make the sleep hormone, melatonin.

The best solution is simply to turn off all screen devices a couple of hours before bed.

Err... um...

LOL. Who am I kidding?

Frankly, I haven't gotten to the point of putting away my technology early in the evening. But I do take several steps to ensure it doesn't wreck my precious sleep.

First, I've set my phone and laptop to "Night Shift" mode, which shifts their displays to warmer colors in the evening.

Second, in the evening, I wear special, blue-blocking glasses to block blue light. The makers of such glasses claim they help melatonin production. These glasses are easy to find at any eyeglasses store or website, or at Amazon (search on "blue light blocking glasses").

Once you're in bed and going to sleep, you want your environment to be *as dark as possible*.

For total darkness, you want Vegas-strength curtains ("blackout" curtains or blinds), or even tape aluminum foil on the windows. The sleep experts say the goal is *zero* light. That includes all those damned LEDs on every single modern electronic appliance. (WiFi routers are the worst! They're like being at a concert!)

My husband goes full blackout on these LED light shows with this amazing stuff called *gaffer's tape*. You can buy it on Amazon. It's magical black tape used in the film industry and by photographers...

he even keeps a small roll in his toiletry kit, along with two clothes-pins, for when we travel, to darken hotel rooms. (The clothespins are to clamp shut unruly window curtains.) Don't have any gaffer's tape? No prob, drape a sock over the alarm clock or other offending light source.

These efforts may seem extreme, but the science has clearly shown that the light from even a single LED dot can negatively affect people's sleep.

Sleep masks are another great way to make sure your sleep environment is dark (more on these, below). And my husband—a night owl who often sleeps during the day—has found that it's easy to make things pitch black just by draping a black t-shirt over his eyes while he sleeps.

Sound & Music

For about a half hour, while I'm getting ready for bed, I listen to special music for inducing sleep called *Sonicaid* (available at Amazon.com, or you can check it out for free on YouTube). I listen to this while washing my face, brushing my teeth, and putting on my nighttime moisturizer... that's part of the ritual, too, my *nighttime* moisturizer, which has its own scent, which I associate with going to bed.

You can imagine how stacking all of these (light, music, behaviors) can really become an entrenched set of sleep triggers.

I turn off the music when I go to bed.

As for sound, you want things quiet, but personally, I make two exceptions:

1. White noise, such as a fan, or a white noise app on my phone, to help cover up sounds that might otherwise bother me, like traffic, loud neighbors, etc.

2. Nature sounds: Ocean waves, rain, babbling brooks, wind in the pine trees, froggy bayou sounds... *I love it all!* So much, in fact, that I often simulate such sounds with the *Oak* meditation app on my phone, or a dedicated device. I use the *HoMedics White Noise Sound Machine*, which is pretty decent, and at $22, it costs a lot less than a beach house on Maui. (They make a portable version of the machine, too.)

Note: Any sound that helps put you to sleep can become habit-forming. To avoid becoming dependent on it, change the sound periodically, and sometimes go without it completely. You want to be able to still fall asleep, even when it's totally silent.

Touch & Temperature

As I mentioned above, sleep masks are another great tool for sleep. They not only block light, but also, *the feeling* of the sleep mask becomes a solid anchor to falling asleep. I'm so used to mine now that I practically drift into sleep the moment I pull it over my eyes!

Sleep masks have come a long way in the past few years. Don't settle for the flimsy crap you sometimes find in hotel freebie kits. Mine is so thick and solid, my husband calls it my "blast shield." (Pretty sure that's a *Star Wars* reference.) Some high-quality sleep masks (see Amazon.com) have bulgy parts that even let you open your eyes in your own, dark little world, which is nice if you don't want to feel anything touching your eyelids.

For good sleep, *be chill*. Literally. Sleep experts say to strive for a temperature of 65 degrees F (18.3 degrees C). I know, sounds brutal, right? Well, you get to use a blanket, and there's something about being swaddled under a thick, snuggly blanket that's extra conducive to deep, restorative sleep. To be clear, I do not always sleep in temperatures this cold... it's difficult during the months that I live in the Arizona desert. But during the winter, it's a reminder to me that it doesn't always need to be toasty warm in the bedroom at night.

Speaking of blankets... you can try a weighted blanket, too. They're believed to stimulate the production of "happiness" hormones like serotonin, and reduce levels of cortisol, the stress hormone. This can help you enter a more relaxed state. These health claims are the subject of ongoing research, but I love my weighted blanket.

Smell & Taste

Smell is a powerful sense to tap into when you want to trigger an anchored response. You know this to be true... when you smell Mom's cookies, you're instantly transported back to childhood. You can do the same for supporting sleep and anchoring certain smells, such as a candle, or like I mentioned above, my special, nighttime-only moisturizer.

I also like using essential oils for this. I keep a bottle of lavender essential oil on my nightstand. At the beginning of my evening ritual, I sit upright on my bed to do Pillow Self-Talk. I add two drops of the lavender to my pillow. This means I'm not only anchoring the smell to sleep, but also to my powerful self-talk!

If you get into the habit of making a special cup of herbal tea two hours or so before bed, after a while, the smell and taste of your tea will become one of the first signals to your body that you're winding down your day.

And before I say more about tea, first, a word about caffeine...

Caffeine

You know I'm a huge fan of coffee. I tie it to my morning self-talk every day. Coffee and self-talk make a powerful combination.

But in the evening, my aim is to have restorative sleep. For that to happen, I need enough *deep* sleep, which occurs during those periods in the night when your brain generates delta brainwaves. The problem is, caffeine messes with your deep sleep. For this reason, I never have caffeine after 1:00 PM. The deep sleep stage is nourishing for your body, mind, and soul. *If your deep sleep gets screwed up, it can affect healing.* And if you don't get enough of this stage of sleep, it can mean not waking truly refreshed. Which can make you cranky and lethargic, and put a twitch in your sparkle. *You don't want your sparkle to twitch!* You want your sparkle on full blast when you wake up!

The timing of caffeine intake is therefore critical. This means watching out not only for coffee, but for any foods and drinks that contain caffeine. Kombucha, chocolate, non-herbal tea, certain supplements, and some pain medications have caffeine in them. Even decaf coffee has a little caffeine, 2mg in a cup (as compared with 95mg with regular coffee).

Ok, back to tea...

Tea Time

Since you won't be drinking coffee in the evening, that leaves a wonderful opening for the next best thing...

Tea!

The more things you reserve as special, "just for bedtime," the more triggers your body has for saying, "Oh, ok, it's time for bed." One thing you can do is to enjoy a cup of tea. Anything herbal will work, from chamomile, to lemon balm, to rooibos—there are many options —but keep whatever variety of tea you choose special for just this purpose: *getting ready for sleep.* Don't drink it at other times of the day. Say to yourself, *This is my special nighttime tea.*

There are two key things to keep in mind with your bedtime tea time. First, the timing. You don't want to drink it too late, or you might have to pee in the middle of the night. I stop drinking all liquids a couple of hours before sleep. So, even though I'm not doing my Pillow Self-Talk during this tea time, I am starting my evening ritual with a small cup of tea a few hours before bed. Which brings me to my second point: Don't drink a super-sized amount, or you'll be in the bathroom all night.

For extra relaxation during evening tea time, consider taking a bath. The warm water, the pampering, the symbolic act of taking time specifically to relax—these are profound for setting yourself up for a magical night of sleep.

I'm not suggesting that you have to do every item in this chapter, or that you have to do any of them every night, but I encourage you to try some different combinations, and see what resonates most with you. Getting this part of your day dialed-in is absolutely worth the effort, and whatever resulting routine you hit upon, your life will improve with reliably good, quality sleep and Pillow Self-Talk.

Bonus Tips for the Best Sleep Ever

Getting enough beautiful, deep sleep contributes greatly to living your best life ever, because you'll feel much better when you're awake. The following are some more tips to make your sleep that much more effective, so you can harness the power of the night to make your dreams come true.

No Alcohol Before Bed

It turns out, the old-school habit of having a nightcap before bed is not a good idea when it comes to sleep quality. We now know that alcohol negatively effects sleep, specifically by disrupting your ability to dream. The REM sleep stage (the state of sleep when you dream) is critical to your health, including your mental health. It's also essential for *manifesting*, because it's during your dreaming state where you can problem solve, come up with new ideas, and think of new things to do. If you're not dreaming, you're not tapping into these awesome benefits of sleep. And if you're one who imbibes close to bedtime and says, "But I still dream," then you'd probably be dreaming *even more* without the alcohol.

Sleep-Tracking Software

If you really want to optimize your sleep, consider getting a sleep tracker app or device. Two years ago, I bought an Oura ring (visit OuraRing.com), and it's one of the best things I've ever bought. It's a cool-looking, shiny black ring that houses a bunch of high-tech sensors that transmit sleep and other health data to an app on your phone. It does *so many cool things*, like track my temperature, such that I know when I'm going to ovulate, and when I'm starting my cycle, based on the tiniest temperature change. It also knows if I might be at risk of getting sick, before symptoms appear, and it warns me to rest. It tracks other things too, like movement and activity. But for me, the best thing *by far* has been the ability to study my sleep, which has led me to experiment with different variables to make my sleep as good as possible.

For example, the Oura ring tracks the different sleep cycles, so I know exactly how much REM and deep sleep I got on any given night. In Italy, I had become accustomed to an afternoon espresso, as is the local custom, and sometimes I was having it as late as 3pm. *Living la dolce vita, sì?*

The curious thing is this... the caffeine didn't affect my ability to fall asleep at night, so I thought I had this new superpower where I could drink caffeine later in the day to boost my brain power for writing my novels, and still fall asleep like a dog at night. But here's the crazy part. Despite falling asleep with no problems, *my deep sleep was negatively affected*, which is not good... I was missing out on restoration, healing, and all kinds of benefits you only get from deep sleep. And I only learned about this deficit because I was tracking it.

The problem was, I didn't know *why* I wasn't getting enough deep sleep. It took me weeks before I realized what was happening. It was the late afternoon espresso. I learned in sleep expert Matthew Walker's masterclass that caffeine affects your deep sleep stage, and when he said that some people don't realize this because "they still fall asleep easily," I was like, *Whoa, is that me?*

I stopped the afternoon caffeine, and voila, my deep sleep returned! I never would've known what was going on without the Oura ring, and who knows how much healing and rest I'd have missed out on. At a minimum, even if you don't get an Oura ring, your deep sleep can be harmed by caffeine consumption too late in the day, and you might not even realize it.

Naps

Don't you just love naps?

I realize that the idea of taking naps might exist only in the realm of pure fantasy, especially for those of us with young children or inflexible work schedules, but know this... naps are really good for you, and even a short nap (15 minutes) can have major cognitive benefits, temporarily juicing your brainpower nearly as much as a full night's sleep.

So if you feel your energy waning, especially if you're a knowledge worker, or if you do creative work, or if you're busting ass working on your plan for manifesting your dream life, then you might actually be *more productive*—or even have the occasional breakthrough, or stroke of genius—as a result of taking a quick power nap, rather than just slogging through when your brain feels like mush.

Naps can give you a huge boost in energy, and it's definitely better than dosing yourself with extra caffeine in the afternoon. But there are some things to keep in mind with napping. For starters, it's best not to nap too late in the afternoon. For me, this means I don't nap after 3:00 PM. Also, the length of a nap is important. A great length for a power-boost nap is 15 to 20 minutes max. You might think you want more, but it's usually better to keep it short. You'll get enough to feel refreshed but not so much that it'll effect your ability to fall asleep later at night, because again, the best thing you can do for your sleep is to stick to a consistent sleep schedule.

Focus Your Bedroom on Two Things

With respect to your sleep environment as a whole, you should also consider using your bed for only two things: sleep and sexy time. If you watch TV in bed, it's confusing to your brain. The bed no longer becomes "the thing you sleep in"… it becomes "the place you hang out." The bed loses its anchor as a sleep trigger! Now, you might think you can anchor watching TV to falling asleep, but nice try, haha. It's too stimulating for falling asleep. And again, all that blue light.

Remember, when you use your bed for only two things, the *feel* of the bed can act as a sleep trigger. Which means, if you're not doing work in bed or watching TV in bed, and you're only sleeping or being romantic, then your body easily makes this connection once you slide between the sheets each night.

Points to Remember

- There is power in having a ritual and an environment to support that ritual.
- Viewing Pillow Self-Talk as your special evening ritual will make you want to do it every night.
- For the best sleep, develop a consistent sleep routine. In particular, try to go to bed at the same time every night, and wake up at the same time every morning.

- Watch the timing of caffeine during the day, and be mindful of alcohol and liquids before bed.
- Make the best environment for your Pillow Self-Talk ritual and sleep by anchoring things to bedtime using your five senses.

CHAPTER 5

HOW TO DO PILLOW SELF-TALK

There is a time for many words, and there is also a time for sleep.

— Homer, The Odyssey

This book is filled with all kinds of great self-talk scripts for different goals and life situations. You might desire more romance or money, or you might want some relaxation after a busy day. Perhaps you seek help with an addiction, or anxiety, or grief. Or maybe you seek direction, or you're just ready to tap into more magical living. Whatever you seek, choose one Pillow Self-Talk script to focus on each night. You might discover that a particular script resonates with you strongly, and in that case, you can repeat it multiple nights in a row. Or, you might prefer to bounce around from one topic to the next each night. It's up to you.

Your Pillow Self-Talk ritual will only take about five minutes each night. Each script is preceded by a brief introduction, which is followed by about twenty lines of self-talk for you to read, out loud, if possible. If you can't read your script out loud, such as if you don't want to disturb your partner who's already asleep, then just mouth the words silently. Mouthing the words is more effective than just reading them.

You may also wish to add your own specific lines of self-talk. You might want to keep a small notebook nearby. (For this purpose, I publish a blank, lined journal that matches this book, the *Pillow Self-Talk Sleep & Dream Journal*, but any plain notebook will work.) And of course, you are always free to write entire scripts for yourself, your own Pillow Self-Talk, and I encourage this. I provide self-talk scripts to give you something to start with. If you resonate with the scripts I've provided, that's great. If there are things you'd like to change about them, then that's great, too.

Relaxed & Focused

Stay focused when you're reading your script. If you catch your mind wandering, simply start over—lovingly, with no judgment—and focus again. Every line of your script should create a picture in your mind. It should also create a nice feeling before you move on to the next line. We all get distracted from time to time. It happens to me, too. I'm always coming up with ideas in the middle of my self-talk rituals, and before I know it, five minutes have gone by before I realize I haven't been fully immersed. So I go back to the beginning. I gladly begin again, with excitement, because I want the fullest effect, the fastest results.

Dr. Joe Dispenza (bestselling author and researcher of epigenetics and neuroscience) writes about how he healed his spinal injury. He was meditating, focusing on his spine, and he would go from top to bottom, through each part of his spine. He was a chiropractor, so he knew all the parts, and he'd visualize each one of them healing. If he got distracted, then he started over at the beginning, and sometimes it took him a very long time to get through his entire spine. But the first time he got through the whole thing without distraction, it was cause for celebration.

And you will feel the same way because, as you practice focusing through this process, your focus actually improves. You'll also find yourself more focused on everything you do in life. Even if you frequently find yourself repeating the first three or four lines of your Pillow Self-Talk script, before you've gotten into the groove of staying focused and relaxed, that's awesome too, because the repetition will give weight to those thoughts in your brain. There's no way to do a bad job with it. It's all good. Repetition is good. And pretty soon, the words you're repeating will be your new normal way of thinking and speaking, to the point where you'll soon never tolerate a bad thought or word about yourself. You'll be struck by just how wrong it feels to say it or think it!

How to Do Your Pillow Self-Talk

You've brushed your teeth and washed your face. You've dimmed the lights, and you're ready for bed. Your evening ritual has begun. You're ready to start.

Step 1. Choose a Pillow Self-Talk script.

When you're deciding which nightly Pillow Self-Talk script to read, don't be overwhelmed by all the options. Anytime you improve one part of your life, other parts improve as well. This means you can jump straight into the section on abundance, or health, or relationships... it doesn't matter where you start, everything gets better because you train your brain to think better and your heart to feel better.

First, select a topic from Part II of the book. Your choices are:

- Star Bright Self-Love
- Astronomical Abundance
- Dazzling Relationships
- Magical Living & Spirituality
- Luminous Health, Healing & Longevity

- Celestial Surrender & Peace
- Eternal Happiness

Once you choose a topic, pick out the script you'd like to use tonight.

Step 2. Sit upright on your bed. Maintain good posture.

Step 3. Read through your chosen Pillow Self-Talk script one or two times (more, if desired). Read it out loud, if possible. If you can't read out loud, then mouth the words silently as you read them.

Step 4. Every few lines, close your eyes, take a slow, calming breath, wait a moment, and feel your relaxation. Feel your elevated state (happy, calm, peaceful, content, relaxed, grateful, etc.). Try to avoid excited emotions (exuberance, joy, etc.), as they may make it difficult to sleep. If you don't feel any elevated emotions, then simply imagine your body being lighter, like it could almost float off the bed. Feeling an elevated emotion is a *very* important part of the Pillow Self-Talk ritual, and it helps get you into a sleepier state. Then, open your eyes and continue repeating the process after a few more lines.

Step 5. At the end of each Pillow Self-Talk script, you will see a choice of three "mantras." Pick one of them, or create your own. This calming mantra is short and sweet, yet empowering. This unique part of the ritual increases its overall impact. It imparts a slightly mystical flavor, as the mantra quiets your brain's monkey chatter. It silences the judgmental regions of the brain and shifts your energy. Keep the mantra in mind; you will use it in a moment.

Step 6. Say your mantra:

- Get comfortable in your bed, in whatever position you like to sleep. Put your book away and turn off the light.
- Rest your head on your pillow. Close your eyes.
- Say your chosen Pillow Self-Talk Mantra to yourself, softly, *but **out loud*** (if possible), TEN times. Do this in a rhythm that feels relaxed and comforting, by taking deep, relaxed

breaths. Say your mantra once, on your in-breath, and once on your out-breath, for five relaxing breaths. Smile softly, and feel elevated feelings of peace, or gratitude, or love, as you say your mantra.

- Next, **mouth** your Pillow Self-Talk Mantra by moving your lips, but this time, it's silent. Follow the same process as before, saying it ten times over five breaths. Mouth it once on an in-breath, and again on the out-breath. As before, feel your lovely, elevated emotion.
- Lastly, you will no longer mouth the mantra. Instead, simply *think* it, over and over, breathing in and breathing out, continuing to do so as you drift off to sleep. Over, and over, and over.

That's it. The entire process only takes a few minutes. A profoundly simple and powerful routine to bring you peace and relaxation, while simultaneously drawing your dreams and goals to you.

Quick Recap

- Read your Pillow Self-Talk script once or twice.
- Say the mantra softly, ten times.
- Mouth the mantra, with no sound, ten times.
- Silently, in your mind, repeat it over and over until you fall asleep.

These are the steps of the Pillow Self-Talk *ritual*. This is important: Don't just read the self-talk lines. Yes, they are lovely and helpful, but *extra mojo* comes when you combine the words with this hypnotic, trance-like exercise with the mantra. It relaxes you more. It helps you fall asleep better and faster. And you feel it getting ingrained deeper into your subconscious, almost like hypnosis. So, bookmark these instructions, in case you need to revisit them a few times until it becomes second nature.

The Next Morning: Creativity Bonus

When you start doing your Pillow Self-Talk ritual, there's another thing you can do upon waking, to take advantage of the creative thoughts that swirled in your mind while sleeping. And that is simply to journal—the moment you wake up—whatever is on your mind, or whatever you remember about your dreams. This simple activity will start your day in a state of *flow*, and before you get caught up running through your to-do's for the day, you can harvest your creativity like it's juicy, low-hanging fruit.

Now, I had always heard about people keeping a dream journal... waking up and writing, first thing... before they even brushed their stinky teeth. Or had a sip of coffee. I was always like, *no way! I'm ready to jump into my day*. But I tried it one day, and honestly, it blew me away. I couldn't believe the stuff coming out of me, like a fire hose... thoughts, insights, story ideas... really creative stuff!

It's now a part of my daily routine. I call it my *Morning Channeling Flow*.

According to Benjamin Hardy, Ph.D, at Inc.com, "Research confirms that the brain, specifically the prefrontal cortex, is most active and readily creative immediately following sleep." So whether it's problem-solving, or writing, or creating music, or figuring out a better way to organize your closet, or coming up with a new idea for a product to sell online... just a few minutes in the morning, to capture your thoughts right when you wake up, could be life-changing for your manifesting.

To do this, keep a journal with blank lines on your nightstand. I also sometimes record voice memos, because I'm not always ready to open my eyes yet, but I'm awake and want to tap into my creative power to capture the connections I made while I slept. I use a little digital voice recorder that makes this super easy. I don't recommend using your phone for this, because the temptation to use the phone for other things is too great, and it'll hijack your flow.

When you journal upon waking, before you do anything else, you take advantage of things happening in your brain from when you slept that you're sometimes not even aware of, because we're ordinarily so quick to check our phones or get up and start the day. But when you start writing before all that gets going, your brain is in its most powerful, creative state. Strike that iron! *It's hot!*

And I'm not just talking about writing down your dreams.

I mean, that's part of it... but there's so much gold—*screw that... diamonds!*—there are so many diamonds to be mined from your mind. The writing can be as quick as two minutes. I have had some of my most blazingly inspired ideas come to me at this time, because I went to sleep with my Pillow Self-Talk, which primed my brain to manifest, or relax me, or to create, and then I wake up on the other side of that sleep, and I harvest those gems.

Sometimes, the strangest thoughts nudge you. And honestly, the stranger the better. That's when I truly feel like I'm channeling something from some external source of knowledge, wisdom, and creativity. The wild ideas are my favorite. They're fun! They have a special magic sauce that can only come from the stars.

Whether it's a dream or something else, just write down whatever is front-and-center in your mind, before your beta brainwaves take over with your daily to-do's. It might be a strange inspiration that suddenly strikes you, or your intuition nudging you to go somewhere or do something. Whatever it is, write it down.

When I'm done writing, *then* I get out of bed.

I say, "I'm going to have an amazing day," as I swing my legs off the bed.

And while I'm brushing my teeth, I say it again, or some other self-love affirmation.

And then, I go have my wonderful coffee, and I do my Coffee Self-Talk.

See how, in this way, your bedtime self-talk routine flows seamlessly into your morning self-talk routine? It's so fun. It's so powerful. *It's so magical.*

Writing Your Own Pillow Self-Talk

Part II of this book contains hundreds of lines of Pillow Self-Talk, covering many facets of life. That may be all you ever want or need. But there are most likely aspects of your life that are unique to you, that are not addressed in the scripts I've provided.

Many people get great value out of writing their own scripts. It can be, not only fun and rewarding, but very effective. The mere act of writing your own scripts requires thought and reflection that can be beneficial to your personal growth. To say nothing of the benefits of repeating those custom-written lines to yourself, every night.

Writing positive self-talk affirmations is not complicated. Essentially, it's just writing sentences about uplifting and positive things that you want *in* your life, and *for* your life. After you've read a few of the examples provided in Part II, you'll start to get a feel for what they sound like.

You may wonder, *What should I write my self-talk about?*

I find it's helpful to start, not with things I want to "fix," but with things that I love. And then write self-talk that's geared toward *expanding* those things in my life. Here are some prompts to get the juices flowing, and help you define your dreams and goals:

1. My favorite pastime is...

2. I love spending time with... (person)

3. In my job, I would love to...

4. My favorite hobbies are...

5. I am most at peace when...

6. I laugh whenever...

7. When I was a kid, I loved...

8. My favorite kinds of books are...

9. If I had all the time in the world, I would...

10. Before I die, I am going to...

Tips for Writing Your Own Pillow Self-Talk

1. Write in First Person

Always write, speak, and think your self-talk in the first person. For example:

I am relaxed and feel peace.

I love my life.

First person is necessary for making "you" both the giver and receiver of the programs that will rewire your brain. It's the easiest way to get straight into your own head and heart, helping you feel the words faster.

2. Write in the Present Tense

Write all of your self-talk as though the thing has already happened, or as though it's happening right now. Not tomorrow, not next month, not next year. Do this even if the thing you want hasn't happened yet. For example:

I am wealthy.

I am fit and healthy. I have the perfect body weight.

Remember, you're doing this to reprogram your brain. You want your brain to start acting *as though the thing you want has already become your reality.* You make your dreams real by thinking about them in the present tense. If you want a life of total freedom with your schedule, then you want to feel free *right now.* If you want wealth and prosperity, then you infuse yourself with feelings of that *right now.*

Some people have a hard time with this. They feel like they're lying to themselves. But it's not lying. This isn't self-deception. It's more like an architect creating a blueprint, or a beautiful drawing of the shimmering skyscraper she has designed. You wouldn't leave a blank spot on the drawing with a note that says, "skyscraper goes here," would you? No, you'd draw the skyscraper and say, "Ok everybody, here's what we're building." You show the *finished product.* That's exactly what self-talk written in the present tense communicates to your subconscious mind. The finished product.

3. Use Elevated Words

Remember that manifesting your dream life will come faster when your thoughts and emotions are in alignment, pulling in the same direction. To do this, choose words and thoughts that make you feel really, *really* good. You're going for: cool, calm, peace, love, gratitude, and/or relaxation. (Reserve the high-energy uplifted feelings, like fun and excitement, for your morning Coffee Self-Talk.)

4. General vs. Specific Self-Talk Statements

In this area, Pillow Self-Talk and Coffee Self-Talk differ slightly. With Coffee Self-Talk, we sometimes get very specific, like targeting a specific number you want in your bank account, or how many rooms are in your dream house. With Pillow Self-Talk, you want to approach it with a more general sense. A *feeling.* Keep your mind open, relaxed, and expansive, like the night sky, filled with stars that glitter like diamonds.

If you focus too much on specific details before bed, it might cause your brain to go into planning mode (beta brainwaves), which might hamper sleep. Save those awesome thoughts for your Coffee Self-Talk the following morning.

5. Rhythm & Flow

When it's evening, we're looking for flowing, expansive, and calm thoughts and feelings. Call on your inner poet to help achieve this. With Pillow Self-Talk, I strategically change the rhythm of the lines, which creates a style that's different from my daytime self-talk. I aim for something almost like a lullaby. Some of my lines rhyme with a poetic and melodic vibe, and I choose words that fit with this approach.

6. Repetition

In the Pillow Self-Talk scripts in Part II, you'll see that some lines are repeated throughout the same script. This is deliberate. The repetition causes them to fire and wire more strongly in your brain, which creates stronger connections.

If you write your own scripts, occasionally repeat the most important lines.

And in almost any script, it's usually a good idea to sprinkle in a few lines about self-love and self-worth, even if that's not the main point of the script. Self-love affirmations are foundational, and they'll make any script more effective.

Points to Remember

- When you're ready to start your Pillow Self-Talk ritual, read your script once or twice. Then say the mantra ten times. Then mouth the mantra ten times. Then repeat it in your mind until you fall asleep.
- Stay relaxed and focused when you do your Pillow Self-Talk. If your mind wanders, simply begin again.
- Journal your dreams and thoughts, first thing upon waking.
- When writing your own Pillow Self-Talk, focus on the things you love and want more of in your dream life.
- Write in the first person, present tense. Use elevated words and spark elevated emotions of calm, peace, love, gratitude and/or relaxation.

PART II
PILLOW SELF-TALK SCRIPTS

STAR BRIGHT SELF-LOVE

The foundation for manifesting the life of your dreams all starts with self-love. Now that we're into the scripts portion of this book, that's where we're going to start.

Let me say it again:

> *The foundation for manifesting the life of your dreams*
> *all starts with self-love.*

Without self-love, you won't feel worthy of living the life of your dreams, and your subconscious will make sure it doesn't happen, or takes longer. Your emotions will not be in sync with your thoughts, and your subconscious will sabotage your efforts.

But once you love yourself, and give yourself permission to live your life on your terms... *whooeee, boy!...* watch out, because your subconscious will start kicking into high gear, and the universe will conspire, moving mountains to make it happen.

The more you experience self-love, the better each day will be. Self-love improves confidence, and excitement, and opportunities in your life. It attracts loving people into your life. It makes you shine brighter. And you experience profoundly deep peace when you possess true self-love.

I wrote the scripts in this section to remind you how amazing you really are. How worthy you are of all your dreams coming true. So dive in, and get cozy with loving yourself.

This section includes the following Pillow Self-Talk scripts for *Star Bright Self-Love*:

- *I Love My Amazing Self*
- *Life Loves Me*
- *I Am Beautiful*
- *Wondrous Self-Worth*

SCRIPT: I LOVE MY AMAZING SELF

The sky grew darker, painted blue on blue, one stroke at a time, into deeper and deeper shades of night.

— HARUKI MURAKAMI

When I started to truly love myself, it was as though a comet burst, and sparks were flying everywhere. I had *thought* I had pretty good self-esteem prior to this, but when I started saying words like the ones in the following script, I quickly discovered how much self-love I had been leaving on the table.

The first thing I noticed was a profound increase in the *gentleness* in my life. My days took on an almost serene feeling. My eyes softened, and my brows ceased to furrow, as I suddenly found myself always with at least a slight smile turning up the corners of my mouth. I was aware of it constantly... it was always just *there*. A warm, happy glow.

Over time, the love expanded. It became richer and more powerful. I walked taller, my face took on a confident air, and my courage rose in proportion to my self-love. And then, magic *really* started to happen in my life.

At least, it felt like magic. My family got happier just witnessing my transformation, and it boosted their own happiness as well. I had more energy to do things. Not just more energy for things that needed to be done, but more energy for play, too. Like impromptu ping-pong games with my daughter. The days of "Not now, I'm too tired," were gone. And my stress drastically reduced. So many things I had previously worried about had seemed worse than they really were because I had lacked overflowing love for myself. Once the love was there, so was a broader perspective. Petty things no longer bothered me, and I was able to focus on the things that really matter.

Pillow Self-Talk Script: I Love My Amazing Self

When I look into the pearly night sky, I fill my mind with dreams of awe and wonder. I love my amazing self.

I am worthy of loving myself and worthy of all the love in the world. Simply because I am. We all are.

I am so thankful that I'm taking time to feel sublime, by loving my own self.

I appreciate myself. I am proud of the steps I'm taking to love myself more.

Tonight, I will fall asleep, loving myself from here to the beautiful moon and back, all night long.

I relax my shoulders, my face shows my state of grace, and I'm calm, because I love myself, and that's all that matters.

Loving myself feels so good. So very, very good.

I have courage, and I'm living my dream life.

I'm madly in love with my life, and it feels so right.

I am dazzled by my own self-love. Look at me go. I did it! I said, "I love me. I am worthy."

Life is amazing, and I am excited to wake up for a new day tomorrow.

I believe in me, because I am magnificent.

I am magical. I am beyond. I am happy.

This is a perfect night to fall asleep loving myself and manifesting while I catch my zzz's.

I am a diamond. I am brilliance. I shine brightly with my own love, and it lights up the world.

I swing from the stars, I bounce on the moon. I am full of love for me, tonight. It fills my magnificent bedroom.

I'm falling into a peaceful slumber, neck and shoulders relaxed, ready for my dreams to come true.

Life is amazing, and I'm grateful for all of it.

Pillow Self-Talk Mantra

Choose one of the following. (See instructions, Chapter 5.)

- *I am deeply in love with me.*
- *I am in love with my life.*
- *My love for me runs deep.*

SCRIPT: LIFE LOVES ME

The sky was so thick with stars, it was as if he could reach out and brush them with his hand.

— JUSTIN CRONIN

It's important to know that Life, the Universe, God, the Force... it's all love, and it all loves you. For my self-talk, I often go back and forth between saying "Life" and "the Universe," but choose whatever word works best for you.

The important thing to know is that *life loves you and adores you,* and it's going to support you, because you are *worthy.* Because your desires are *meant for you.* Everything you want to do and attract will come to you when you think and feel the right energy to make it happen.

So when you fall asleep tonight, rest easy, knowing and feeling your dream life is coming to you, because life loves you. Always come to bed from a place of love, and the world can't help but conspire to join you. It's a comforting feeling.

Pillow Self-Talk Script: Life Loves Me

It's a lovely night tonight, and my heart is full of kindness and love as I fall asleep. Life loves me so much.

The stars above shine, shine, shine, and my dreams are all mine.

I love life, and life loves me... hugging me, high-fiving me, and supporting my everything.

I am grateful for all the love in my life.

Life supports me, and I am drawing my dreams to me, because I am full of love. Life loves me so much.

I fall asleep tonight, peaceful, supported by life's love for me. It's always there.

Everywhere I look, life is ready to give me a boost.

I ride with life through the star-blazing night, confident that I'm loved and supported, and all is right.

My arms are open to receive, and I welcome all the help that life has for me.

I am never alone, because life loves me.

My passion for life sparkles and twinkles like the stars. I'm living the best life ever. Thank you, Life. Thank you, ME!

I love myself, and I appreciate the steps I am taking to live a more magnificent life. I am worthy.

I have freedom to be my true self, and this expands me.

I am full of ideas, bursting with them like a full moon. My pearly light shines through the night. Life loves me.

All is well, and I'm tapping into my own beautiful, shining soul. I am smart. I am kind. I am epic.

When I close my eyes tonight, the moon high in the sky, I feel peace, and love, and generosity.

I trust in the Universe and Life with all my heart. They always answer. They always deliver.

It is safe to follow my truth and trust life. Life loves me so much.

I appreciate me.

I enjoy taking time in the evening to relax my mind. I'm worthy of my magical dreams coming true.

Tonight, I luxuriate in peace, love, and the gifts that life has coming to me.

Pillow Self-Talk Mantra

Choose one of the following. (See instructions, Chapter 5.)

- *I love life, and life loves me.*
- *I am happy and free to be me.*
- *I shine, and my dreams are mine.*

SCRIPT: I AM BEAUTIFUL

His hair had clearly been up all night, having adventures without him.

— RACHEL HARTMAN

Tonight's self-talk is about beauty. It's inside and outside every one of us. We are all beautiful and all unique in our colors of skin, textures of hair, shapes of our faces, eyes, and noses, and the way we carry our bodies.

Beauty is everywhere! And here's an amazing truth... you will see more beauty around you when you start with seeing the beauty in *yourself*. Remember, say the following script, even if you don't believe everything it says about you yet. That's ok. Over time, it will gradually become your truth; your brain will listen to you. So just say it, and keep saying it, and watch the glow of your shimmering soul unfold.

Fun story! We had a member in our Coffee Self-Talk Facebook group post to the group, saying that she told herself "I am pretty," over and over, on her way to work one day. She didn't actually believe she was pretty, but she said it anyway. And that day at work, multiple people told her how pretty she looked! She said that had never happened before.

The mind makes it true. You give off a beautiful vibe, and people are attracted to it.

And she's not alone. I get emails like this all the time.

It works. Try it for yourself.

Pillow Self-Talk Script: I Am Beautiful

I am beautiful. So very, very beautiful.

My soul shines, and it lights up my face. I radiate beauty, inside and out.

I am wonderful, attractive, and my energy is awe-inspiring.

I love to smile, and it attracts my dreams and goals to me faster. I am beautiful, inside and out.

Smiling people attract other smiling people. It's a magical way to live.

Everything is going my way, and it always will, because I am the master conductor of my life.

Joy bubbles up inside me, creating beauty all around me.

I swirl and twirl and relax into my beautiful self, as the night beckons with peace.

Thank you, gorgeous body, for taking care of me. I am beautiful inside and out.

My body is strong and beautiful, and I have health all around me.

I see beauty everywhere, every day, from the moment my eyes open, to the moment they close at night.

I love my life, and my life loves me. I am making my dreams come true.

The universe is open for me, with unlimited possibility.

When I look in the mirror, a beautiful me looks back.

Effortless sleep is my specialty, and I welcome my dreams with open arms, drawing them to me, attracting a life of bliss and beauty.

I appreciate the beauty that I witness all over the world, from all the different people and cultures. Life is amazing, and we are one.

I love life. I love sleep. I love me.

My soul is soothed by sleep. Sweet, healthy, peaceful sleep.

I am wild with love, because I cherish my beauty, inside and out.

I love my eyes, my eyelashes, my eyebrows, and my ears. I love my hands and feet. I love me.

I am kind and generous with myself and others.

The sultry darkness of the night shelters me and comforts me, and I prepare for the deepest, most amazing sleep.

I am a perfect vibrational match for my desired dreams, and they're coming to me.

I'm falling asleep with positive thoughts about me, my body, and my life.

I am beautiful, inside and out.

Pillow Self-Talk Mantra

Choose one of the following. (See instructions, Chapter 5.)

- *I am beautiful and full of love.*
- *I am full of peace and beauty.*
- *I shine because my dreams are mine.*

SCRIPT: WONDROUS SELF-WORTH

Owning our story and loving ourselves through that process is the bravest thing that we'll ever do.

— Brené Brown

The world can only see us as we see ourselves. This is critical for living your most magical life because, when we shine, people shine back. And what makes you shine? Feeling worthy. Feeling so much worth for your heart, your soul, your health, your success, your everything... that an extraordinary knowing courses through your veins. You feel it whispering in your bones,

"I am worthy. I am wonderful. I am magical. I am here to play at the highest level."

The world responds and treats us as we treat ourselves. So start tonight, exploring the wondrous world of self-worth, and watch the shadows fade and your light shine. Feel the strength of the new you, being the hero of your own life, wielding your own magic wand and sword. You have unbelievable power. *You are wondrous.*

When you feel worthy, you will be amazed at how effortless your life feels. You become more generous with yourself and others. You forgive yourself and others. You love yourself and others.

Get ready to transform into something amazing when your tank is full of self-worth.

I will say simply this: *You are worthy.*

We all are.

Pillow Self-Talk Script: Wondrous Self-Worth

I am worthy of living the most epic life. I am supported in all ways, beginning with me.

My self-worth is powerful, and it opens doors of opportunities for me.

I rest easy and have peace all around me, because I connect with my truth and self-worth.

I am worthy. We are all worthy. We are all on this spaceship ride of life together.

The passionate fire of my day slides into the glowing embers of the night, where I rest and recharge.

When I show up to life feeling worthy, it allows other people to show up to life feeling worthy, too. We are all one.

I rest easy, full of peace, and my dreams are coming true. I am worthy.

I experience inner greatness. I'm full of love, and life, and power.

I close my eyes and feel the energy of flow. I am worthy of happiness, peace, love. Thank you, Life, for today.

I love my life, because it has direction and meaning. I am unlimited, full of potential, and ready to fly amongst the stars in my sleep tonight.

I have an abundance of beautiful time. I am worthy of everything.

My life is a journey, and I'm ever-growing and developing, becoming my own magnificent self. I love this new me.

I am making the world a happier place, one smile at a time.

Prosperity is all around me, and I'm transforming into something incredible and amazing. I am worthy.

I stay loose, relaxed, and I let down my hair. It's time to shift into a calm evening.

It's my time to own my life.

I love taking care of myself, and I keep my life in order while remaining open to the unexpected blessings ready to rain down on me.

I was born knowing my way. I reconnect with my self tonight.

The evening dazzles with promises of beautiful dreams. I am worthy.

The night sky glows with hope and love. The stars are like charms all around me.

My spirit soars like a glimmering shot to the moon, because I am my own hero.

My dreams take on momentum, and everything in my life is getting better and better.

Sweet dreams, my sweet love, sweet dreams.

Pillow Self-Talk Mantra

Choose one of the following. (See instructions, Chapter 5.)

- *I am worthy of peace.*
- *I am worthy of wealth.*
- *I am worthy of love.*

ASTRONOMICAL ABUNDANCE

Most people associate "abundance" with money, which is understandable. But I find this to be much too narrow for such a fantastic concept. When I do my self-talk, and I think of the word *abundance*, I apply it to a few different categories, such as:

- Abundance of money and prosperity
- Abundance of energy
- Abundance of time
- Abundance of health

Abundance is a rich word. It conjures pictures of overflowing, spilling over, waterfalls. It brings the feeling of relaxation because, with abundance, there is always *more than enough*. No lack, no survival emotions, just abundance. When you know you have an abundance of time, you're relaxed. When you have an abundance of health, you're relaxed. When you have an abundance of money, you're relaxed.

In short, it means you have *more than enough* of everything that you need.

So, go ahead and tie the thought and feeling of abundance to anything you like: time, money, creativity, beauty, health, confidence, self-love, etc. If you want to attract that type of abundance, you want to picture it and feel it now.

Ask yourself: *What does abundance feel like?*

You might wonder, *How can I know what it feels like to be rich if I'm not rich?* And it's a good question. But keep in mind, you're accomplishing many things with your elevated thoughts and feelings. So if you want riches, then do what you can internally with your thoughts and feelings to *pretend* you are rich. You want to think so profoundly, *as if you are*, that your brain believes it, and you put out a beautiful, high-vibing energy that starts drawing your abundance to you.

It all starts with your thoughts and feelings, your laser focus. Do this regularly, and then watch as you begin to see new opportunities for abundance all around you. The point is to simply *feeeeel amazing*, and that feeling comes in many flavors, any of which are powerful for creating your magical dream life.

This section includes the following Pillow Self-Talk scripts for *Astronomical Abundance*:

- *Prosperity Is My Destiny*
- *Overflowing Creativity*
- *All the Time in the World*
- *Effortless Energy*

SCRIPT: PROSPERITY IS MY DESTINY

I'm hungry for a juicy life. I lean out my window at night, and I can taste it out there, just waiting for me.

— Brigid Lowry, Guitar Highway Rose

Tonight's Pillow Self-Talk is about abundance in the usual way people think of it: Prosperity. In other words... a lot of money.

When it comes to prosperity and money, you might be in a situation where you could use a heck of a lot more. This is a great script to *get your mind in the mood for massive moola*. Think about, and picture in your mind, what inspires you regarding prosperity.

What does that look like for you?

Is it a big number in your bank account? Does it mean having more clients? Is it a bigger house? Receiving a check in the mail? Or finding a box of gold bars on your doorstep? That last one might seem a little silly, but playful energy and vivid images are great for visualizing abundance.

Whatever mind picture you choose, think of something that represents prosperity to you, and take a moment, feeling how relaxed and incredible you feel with this abundance of prosperity in your life. Notice how it feels so good.

Tap into that good feeling, and understand that the best energy for attracting money and opportunities is to feel relaxed and uplifted. In doing so, you place your own worthy self solidly on the same elevated plane that you place money, thereby making it easier to obtain, and a natural fit in your life.

Pillow Self-Talk Script: Prosperity Is My Destiny

Money is all around me, and it is easy to get. Relax, baby, relax.

Prosperity is coming to me in the night sky, while I sleep. Relax, baby, relax.

My income is increasing, and good times lie before me. Relax, baby, relax.

My treasured desires are my lavish destiny. Sparkle, twinkle, pop.

I am prosperous, because I am worthy of prosperity. Relax, baby, relax.

I radiate love, I radiate life, and my energy draws abundance and wealth to me like a magnet.

It is safe to want all the money that I want. I am honored to receive. Relax, baby, relax.

I will have a peaceful sleep tonight, because I'm calm. The momentum of magnificence starts right now.

Money is easy to get, and it's around me, all the time. It's everywhere. I just have to open my eyes and see. There's more than enough.

I love thinking and feeling abundance. It's like sleeping on a bed of roses, a mattress stuffed with cash.

I am wild with prosperity, and I love me. Tea bags full of diamonds? Yes, please. I'll take that, too.

Money and abundance respond to my thoughts and feelings about it. Relax, baby, relax.

I flipped the switch to feeling abundance. I now glow with this knowing.

I attract all the money I want. I lounge with ease. I can slow down when I want, as there are always plenty of opportunities.

The cool darkness of the night is beautiful, supple and soft, and it curves around me, tendrils of peace, as I sleep.

I am rich, rich, rich with abundance and prosperity. Relax, baby, relax.

When the sun sets, I am grateful for everything that comes next—the black sky, the moon, the stars, and the quiet spirit of the night.

I was born for this. The riches I seek also seek me.

My life is amazing, and I am grateful for all the money coming my way. Relax, baby, relax.

Being prosperous is easy for me and I shimmer and shine with creativity and individuality.

I am worthy of everything my heart desires. Prosperity loves me.

I am drifting to sleep, nestled in the pink clouds of the night.

Relax, baby, relax.

Pillow Self-Talk Mantra

Choose one of the following. (See instructions, Chapter 5.)

- *I am wealthy, I am wealthy, I am wealthy.*
- *Waves of peace wash over me.*
- *I love money, and money loves me.*

SCRIPT: OVERFLOWING CREATIVITY

Imagination is everything. It is the preview of life's coming attractions.

— ALBERT EINSTEIN

This script applies to everyone, because having an abundance of creativity is helpful for anybody. It's not just for people who think of themselves as "creative." Creativity is about approaching things in new ways. It's about being *clever*. Or *different*. Whether you are an artist, or a problem-solver who loves to think outside-the-box, or just a beautiful individual making your way in the world, life is always easier when your creative genius is easy to access.

Sleeping is one of the best ways to tap into this source of genius that we all possess. When you sleep, your analytical brain takes a break (it's literally asleep), which allows all the crazy, unfiltered, uncensored ideas from your wacky, brilliant subconscious to bubble up to the surface.

So get a journal ready (see Chapter 5). For the next *eleven days*, every morning, just write some notes—*first thing*—when you wake up, and see what kind of awesome stuff comes out of you. See what you unleash!

(If you cure cancer, give me a shout-out at your Nobel acceptance speech, ok?)

It's time to dive into having an abundance of creativity. Remember to tailor these lines to suit you and your own specific creative dreams.

Pillow Self-Talk Script: Overflowing Creativity

I shimmer like the stars, full of creativity. I overflow and glitter, and I sparkle with inspiration.

When I sleep, my brain solves problems. Creativity is mine.

I give myself permission to live my exquisite life.

I am always full of ideas, my creativity well is overflowing. If I draw a bucket of inspiration, it's immediately replenished.

Ideas come easily to me. There are always more where they came from.

All is one, and I'm filled with deep joy.

The more I tap into my creativity, the more I have.

I love my creativity, and my creativity loves me.

I invent in my dreams.

I love feeling creative, and I have an abundance of it for solving problems, seeing things in new light, and living my best life.

I am falling asleep with creative thoughts.

I easily align myself with innovation, and I love learning new skills. Yeah, I'm pretty much awesome.

The lush tapestry of my dreams brings me creativity during the night.

My life is magnificent, because I make it so.

I solve problems in my sleep. I am loved deeply and daily from life.

I have vision and inspiration... it swirls all around me. I love being expressive.

My sleep is filled with artistry, and I wake up each morning, ready to take creative action.

I have faith and courage in my individuality, and I shine.

My inspiration is unleashed in my dreams, and I wake refreshed, excited, and full of amazing ideas.

I'm grateful for everything in my life.

Ideas for innovation come to me in my sleep with a Big Bang, and I love the night for this.

I rest easy tonight, relaxed, knowing my dreams are working for me behind the scenes.

Pillow Self-Talk Mantra

Choose one of the following. (See instructions, Chapter 5.)

- *The answers are coming to me.*
- *I am a prolific writer.*
- *I am a creative genius.*

SCRIPT: ALL THE TIME IN THE WORLD

The two most powerful warriors are patience and time.

— Leo Tolstoy

This is one of my favorite scripts. When I think about all the different ways I could be prosperous, it often involves lots of projects and a shit ton of things to do. As any business owner knows, you can always be doing more. For me, whether that means writing the next book, or creating an online course, or interfacing with more readers on social media, there's always something I could be doing. There's always a way I can move, dance, and flow to attract more opportunities. And, of course, I want time for my family, and friends, and exercising, and reading, and *me time*, and on and on...

So many opportunities! It could become stressful thinking about *how in the world to do it all?*

That's where I stop and take a breath. I soften my shoulders and close my eyes. I relax and slip into a lovely Pillow Self-Talk script that reminds me... *"Oh darling, I have an abundance of time to do everything I want."*

Oh, yeah.

That's right.

I do.

I *do* have an abundance of time. It's just that, sometimes, I get so excited with projects, wondering when it'll all get done. But I tell you, just saying the awesome affirmation—"*I have an abundance of time*"—relaxes my whole body with a loungy-vibe, all velvety and soft like my old, favorite track suit.

I want you to open your mind if you ever feel harried or like a raging woodpecker. Open your mind like the roof of your house has just lifted off. Repeat the affirmation below about *having an abundance of time,* and watch how you magically do. Whether your life has five things or fifty-five things going on, your time is abundant. Overflowing. You have more than enough time to *get it all done.*

How does this work?

The subconscious mind does magic. It just *makes it happen.*

And so it is with this idea, that you focus tonight's Pillow Self-Talk on having an abundance of time. When you start to see all the opportunities coming to you, or you start to have so many ideas that you run out of sticky notes and napkins just to write them on, rest easy... time is overflowing for you.

Remember this: You're unavailable for feelings of scarcity or lack, because you are living your legendary life, on your time, on your terms. *Time is your BFF.*

Pillow Self-Talk Script: All the Time in the World

My day is turning into night, and everything is going so very, very right.

The journey is amazing, and the steps I take are filled with calm.

I love to smell the roses, and I have an abundance of time to do it. Sniff. Sniff.

I have plenty of time to sleep as long as I need. I am love.

I am filled with creativity, and opportunities, and ideas, and it is wonderful because I have an abundance of time to do everything I want.

I have courage and momentum for all of the magical opportunities coming my way.

I love time, and time loves me.

I am at peace, because I have time to do everything on my to-do list.

I am relaxed.

I am worthy of taking my time.

I am wealthy with time.

I have an abundance of time to do everything I want. Ahhhhhh, it feeeeeels soooooo good.

I am a mighty queen/king, and my dreams reign supreme.

I have more than enough time to complete all of my projects with ease and peace.

I have an abundance of beautiful time.

I am doing everything that I want to be doing.

I am in the right place, at the right time, doing the right thing.

My life is full of calm energy. I am calm. I am legendary.

I am doing what I want, because I have an abundance of time to do it all.

Time is effortless for me, and I breathe easily.

I am relaxed, and I relax into calm energy, because I have time.

Overflowing time, that's how I roll. Overflowing time, baby.

I have plenty of time to sleep, and I am worth it.

Everywhere I look, I have an abundance of time.

The sun rises, and I have time. The sun sets, and I have time.

I'm ready for sleep now. Deep breath. I have an abundance of time.

Pillow Self-Talk Mantra

Choose one of the following. (See instructions, Chapter 5.)

- *I have an abundance of time.*
- *I have time for everything I want to do.*
- *I am worthy of time.*

SCRIPT: EFFORTLESS ENERGY

The sky is already purple; the first few stars have appeared, suddenly, as if someone had thrown a handful of silver across the edge of the world.

— ALICE HOFFMAN

Similar to the previous Pillow Self-Talk script, *All the Time in The World*, sometimes you want more *energy*, too. It's time to manifest an abundance of energy. But not so much buzzy energy that you can't sleep!

When I say "energy," I mean two different types of the stuff. There's the physical kind, to get everything done that you want to get done in a day. But I also mean an abundance of *elevated vibrational energy*. Your frequency. Your bitchin' *success vibe*. This script works for both types.

Pillow Self-Talk Script: Effortless Energy

I have an abundance of energy, and it swirls and twirls through me, and around me, all through the night. Energy loves me.

I stay on top, and I call the shots. I love energy, and energy loves me.

All is well.

The magic of the night embraces me as I recharge my body for another brilliant day.

My positive energy shoots like stars and twinkles all around me, and everybody else.

My amazing, elevated energy is so abundant that it attracts other people and inspires them.

I glitter and glisten with beautiful energy.

I have an abundance of energy to do everything I want to do.

The night gently swirls with peace all around me.

Everything works in my favor. I am expansive.

There's so much abundance in the universe that there is more, and more, and more.

I am relaxed. So very, very relaxed. My energy is amazing, and I fly through my day soaring with beautiful, precious, loving energy. Recharging by night.

I stand in my own peace, at the edge of my dreams.

I have an abundance of energy to do everything I desire.

My zeal sparkles all around me.

I always have more than enough energy to fulfill my dreams.

My elevated energy attracts everything I want.

Uplifted energy is effortless for me, and it draws my desires to me.

Energy is beautiful, and I am beautiful.

I am living my best life and filled with gratitude for everything in it.

My life is the stuff dreams are made of.

Pillow Self-Talk Mantra

Choose one of the following. (See instructions, Chapter 5.)

- *I radiate a beautiful vibration.*
- *I have all the energy I need.*
- *My dreams are filled with loving energy.*

DAZZLING RELATIONSHIPS

Relationships are essential to the human experience. They are important for health, longevity, and happiness. Even so, sometimes life gets busy, and relationships can be taken for granted, and they are sometimes the first things to get bumped to the side. With the scripts in this section, you'll inject new adventure and love into this part of your life, and your life will blossom as a result.

It all starts with the relationship you have with yourself. It's the foundation for living a magical life, and it sets the tone for all of the relationships in your life, whether at work, or at home, or in the community at large.

This section includes the following Pillow Self-Talk scripts for *Dazzling Relationships***:**

- *Me, Myself, and I*
- *Passionate Partners*
- *Peaceful Parenting*
- *Fabulous Friendships*

SCRIPT: ME, MYSELF, AND I

A cool breeze stirred my hair at that moment, as the night wind began to come down from the hills, but it felt like a breath from another world.

— FRANCIS MARION CRAWFORD

Tonight's Pillow Self-Talk is about you.

You. You. YOU!

Your relationship with *you* sets the tone for all other relationships. The way you treat yourself will largely affect *how others treat you.* So if you want to have amazing, other-worldly-awesome relationships, then you must start with the relationship you have with yourself, and make it awesome, too.

It's incredible to watch yourself grow, as you love yourself more with your self-talk. The profound transformations that happen will challenge everything you ever thought you knew about life. You will see things differently, as your self-love shines outward on the world around you. You begin to realize how much love you get *from other people.* Including strangers!

Of course, some of the relationships in your life may be less than ideal. As your self-love grows, you might outgrow some of these relationships, and that's ok. If this happens, just keep shining, and see if these people grow too, and become a part of your joyful vibe.

When you spend time with someone, you'll start to pay attention to how you feel in your heart when you're around them. What is your energy like? Does it shift higher? Or lower? And when your interaction with that person is over, whether in person, via email, online, or over the phone, do you feel uplifted? Or drained?

It's perfectly fine to choose to be with people who fill your cup. And vice versa! You want to shine, and love so brightly that their cup is filled effortlessly too, just by *you being you*. And this happens when you have abundant self-love. So, let's dive in!

Pillow Self-Talk Script: Me, Myself, and I

I love me, and I am a wonderful, kind person.

I love to grow, and my relationship with myself improves every day.

I appreciate me and the time I put into making my life better.

I am on a magic carpet ride, and love is all around me.

I shine bright, and I allow others to shine their light.

It is fun taking care of myself and loving me. I'm worth it.

I am magical. I am legendary. I am beyond.

I love life, and life loves me. I love me!

I am the hero of my night. Thank you, Life, for today.

I am born from a star, and I shine brilliantly.

I am honored to love myself.

All is wonderful this evening.

I am open-minded, and I shine with love, like a trillion magical stars.

I am grateful for the privilege to live such an amazing life. I pay attention to my relationships, and I make sure they're uplifting my soul.

I dance my dance, loose and fun. I'm spirited, I'm brave, a moonshot of momentum.

My dreams bloom and blossom in the night like jasmine.

I am the queen/king of my mind, and it does my bidding for me. I direct it, and it follows my lead.

The wonders of the night soothe my mind as I drift to sleep. I'm ready for my dreams. I'm happy to be me.

My loving self-talk is guaranteed to give me a better life. I know it. I feel it. I'm living it.

I am genuine, blessed, and calm. I love my life.

I take the time to love myself, because it's the most important ingredient to living my best life.

I'm open to all that the night has to offer as I drift into dreamland.

It's time to rest, time to sleep. I close my eyes and enter deep peace.

Pillow Self-Talk Mantra

Choose one of the following. (See instructions, Chapter 5.)

- *I love my life.*
- *I love myself. I am worthy.*
- *My life is magical.*

SCRIPT: PASSIONATE PARTNERS

Night time

You'll find her there

Blooming

Like a night rose.

— Melody Lee

If you want more love in your relationship, you need to *put more love into it*. You make it a *priority*. And a great way to start is with self-talk.

If your relationship could use a love boost, then start with you. Don't start with him or her. Start with you, and your own love and happiness. I hear from readers all the time telling me that their relationships improved when they started with themselves, and their partner couldn't help but notice the dramatic changes that were happening.

Use this script to keep the sizzle and juices flowing.

Pillow Self-Talk Script: Passionate Partners

I smile whenever I think about my partner.

I overflow with support for my partner's interests and passions.

I feel safe with my partner.

My soul harmonizes with my partner's.

We are on the most incredible magic carpet ride ever, soaring through the night sky, filled with a trillion sparkling stars.

My partner and I love to be honest with each other, and support each other, in everything we want to do.

I love kissing my partner. I love making my partner feel good.

I feel incredible and amazing. I spread my love to my partner, on my partner, and with my partner.

I like to touch my partner whenever I pass by. These little affections constantly let him/her know how much I love him/her.

When my lover talks to me, I give him/her my undivided attention, and it feels good to be so focused on him/her.

As nighttime falls, my heart expands with more and more love for my partner.

I love falling asleep with my partner. Our love intertwines, twisting, warm, and luminous.

I create passionate energy with my intentions of love for my partner.

We are relaxed, and our love feels so good. I am ready for romance.

My heart is safe with my partner, and my partner's heart is safe with me.

Every night when I fall asleep next to my partner, I fall asleep with a smile.

Every morning when I wake up with my partner, I smile with gratitude.

We enjoy romantic meals and walks, and we talk about our dreams together.

Our romance is star-like, dazzling and bright. We have amazing new adventures coming our way in our dreams tonight.

Our life is full of love, warmth, and respect. We have the most incredible future ahead of us. Our dreams intersect.

I love living life with my partner. We are shipmates. Co-pilots.

We love laughing, and we love doing new things together. Our life is one thrilling adventure.

All is wonderful tonight. The stars shine, and we relax. I am relaxed.

I know that anything is possible with my marvelous partner.

Our days and nights are full of love, joy, and passion.

Pillow Self-Talk Mantra

Choose one of the following. (See instructions, Chapter 5.)

- *I love (fill in your partner's name here) so much.*
- *Our life is an amazing adventure.*
- *I love our life together.*

SCRIPT: PEACEFUL PARENTING

Peace begins with a smile.

— MOTHER TERESA

Raising children is one of the greatest opportunities in the human experience, and this script will help you increase your patience, excitement, and wonder for the whole process. You can tailor this self-talk to include the specific names of your kiddo(s), which I recommend. This script alternates between singular and plural (kid/kids, child/children), so just modify it to fit your family.

Pillow Self-Talk Script: Peaceful Parenting

It's time to unwind, and my soul rests with ease. I love my family so much, we have so much peace.

My family and I are on a sparkling, grand adventure. We're flying through the night sky on a magic carpet ride.

When my child comes into the room looking for me, I give my him/her my undivided attention.

I love my children, and they love me. When I listen to them, I show them that they have a voice worthy of being heard.

I have sweet dreams about my children. I am ready for a night of beautiful sleep.

Playful parenting is my passion. I love making my kids giggle and laugh.

The stars twinkle over my family as we get ready for bed. I am so grateful for them. I love my life.

I adore snuggling with my family. It warms my soul. I am at peace, and peace is all around me.

We are creative geniuses in my family. We love to learn, and we're filled with fun questions.

If there's something I don't know the answer to, I look it up. I teach this skill and habit to my children, too.

My family is healthy, and happy, and bright with enthusiasm.

I fall asleep full of love every night. I am filled with peaceful patience.

I am a great role model for my kids. We are blessed. We are inspired.

My kids feel safe to ask any question at any time. I love teaching my family.

I remain focused on what matters: happiness, joy, and love.

I honor my child as an individual, and I support his/her passions.

My soul bursts with thankfulness and appreciation for my children.

I have patience and kindness in my heart, and I allow my children to do things in their own time.

I love spending time with my child. Being a parent is a precious role in life. I honor it.

I support my kids' dreams and desires, and they support mine. They are worthy. I am worthy. We are all worthy.

We live healthy lives. We live a phenomenal, legendary life, and I relax into peaceful sleep, knowing my children are safe and happy.

My child and I love to smile and wink at each other.

I am happy to show my children respect, which teaches them to respect me.

When I need time for myself, I love myself and take it. It makes me a better parent when I do this.

My own self-love teaches my kids how to love themselves.

I am ready for sleep. I am relaxed. I take a deep breath full of gratitude. I am tucking myself in right now, surrounding myself with all the love of the stars, the love of myself.

Pillow Self-Talk Mantra

Choose one of the following. (See instructions, Chapter 5.)

- *I am a kind parent.*
- *I am a patient mom/dad.*
- *We love our life.*

SCRIPT: FABULOUS FRIENDSHIPS

But I look up above and see the sky

With the moon and stars capturing my eye

I know that you can see it too

Cuz no matter where you are, the sky remains true.

— Talia Basma

How incredible is it to have a BFF? Isn't it wonderful when you know someone always has your back, no matter what? And how fun is it when you're enjoying time with your best friends? The time flies, and it's filled with laughter, trust, support, and just a super great time. Memories get made.

When you're on the *Magical Life Train*, your community can have a big impact on your success. Use this script to enhance the awesome friendships you already have, and to attract even more relationships like that.

Pillow Self-Talk Script: Fabulous Friendships

I love my friends, and they love me.

Time with my friends is precious. We trust each other.

My friends and I have each other's backs, and we are always there for each other, no matter what.

I am always excited to see my friends.

I am filled with love, and I welcome amazing friendships into my life.

I love to hug my friends. We are so very close.

I trust my friends, and they trust me.

My best friend and I have the most beautiful relationship, filled with love and fun adventures.

I attract good friends with big hearts.

I am relaxed tonight. I smile, thinking about my friends.

My friends uplift me, and I uplift them.

I am grateful for my best friends.

I have amazing opportunities for friendships all around me.

I am worthy of the most amazing and loyal friendships.

I am excited to support my friends and their passions.

My circle of friends is a circle of safety.

It's easy to make time for my friends, and it makes life more magical to do so.

When I allow others to live their own truth, the whole world brightens, like a full moon guiding us through the night.

My friends and I love to hang out. We're relaxed around each other. We're good to each other. We can feel the love in the air.

I feel terrific about my friendships. I am grateful for my friends.

I have an incredible attitude tonight, and I'm going to have incredible dreams, which will make for an incredible tomorrow.

I am falling asleep with friendly and fun thoughts tonight. Good night.

Pillow Self-Talk Mantra

Choose one of the following. (See instructions, Chapter 5.)

- *I have amazing friends.*
- *I am a great friend.*
- *My friends and I love making memories together.*

MAGICAL LIVING & SPIRITUALITY

This section is perfect for helping you dip into the divine. *Going beyond* in your mind. All things magical and mystical.

Whether you believe in God, or the Universe, or Life's Flow, or the Tao, or Oneness, or Gaia, or the Wee Folk, or nothing at all, this is an amazing way to explore the depths of this beautiful and powerful part of life. The following scripts offer sparkling peace, and inspiration that seems to glitter around you and inspire incredible dreams.

This section includes the following Pillow Self-Talk scripts for *Magical Living & Spirituality*:

- *Manifesting My Magical Life*
- *All Is Well*
- *We Are One*
- *The Great, Sparkling Galaxy*

SCRIPT: MANIFESTING MY MAGICAL LIFE

When the twilight sun is sinking, dusk embraces Mother Earth. What a joy to catch the splendor, moments of unmeasured worth.

— GRETA ZWAAN

Manifesting a magical life is pure fun. You get to be happy... pretty much all the time. Pillow Self-Talk helps by shifting your mindset as you wind down each night and get ready to sleep. It gets you excited about twinkling stars, dreams, and endless possibilities. You even get the peace and health benefits that come from improving your sleep.

Manifesting a magical life is actually very easy. It does take commitment and belief though. Believe it works, believe in the power of your mind, and that's when you take control. It could be the biggest turning point in your life, simply by thinking and feeling magical, empowered, and full of love. Ideas and inspirations appear, and you dance with them.

The more often you embrace this attitude, the more magical your life will be, and the faster your dreams will become reality. My default mindset is this: *magic, love, and happiness.* The longer I focus on these, the better it gets. Unbelievably better. *Insanely better!* The moment I think I'm at the pinnacle and can't climb any higher... *it still gets better.*

It also gets easier. It gets easier because I've trained my brain to be this way. It becomes habit. Second nature. Effortless. You become so self-aware that the tiniest signal gets your attention, and you take action.

This all happens because I do the work. If you do the work, it will happen for you, too.

I am deliberate in my living. I am focused on my goal of happiness and abundance. I have found a state of mind that literally gives everything a magical quality, a kind of sparkle. It makes everything fun, and everything exciting. I've truly manifested a magical life, and this script will help you do it, too.

Pillow Self-Talk Script: Manifesting My Magical Life

I love life, and life loves me.

My cells and bones glow with passion for my magical life.

Confidence is my comfort zone. I slide into it with the ease of sliding between my cool, comfy sheets.

It's a lovely night tonight. It's a great time to sleep. I sleep easily. I rest simply.

My dreams are full of spiraling magic that whirls in the wind, and my dreams feel good.

My heart rests easy, and I am living an amazing life.

I'm an amazing manifester. I manifest even while I'm sleeping.

I trust in the Universe. Life's Flow. It always delivers. I do my part, and Life does its part.

Intuition flows through my veins, glittering with promise, and I follow its lead.

I feel peace right now, in this very moment, because I'm taking care of me. I deserve this time in the evening to prepare for my night and make it the best sleep ever.

I am falling asleep with magical thoughts and feelings, and these things draw my life's dreams to me.

I dance boldly in the direction I'm attracting, and I show the Universe I'm here, ready to receive.

My life is expanding with abundance and opportunities in every eternal moment.

I feel loved, deeply and daily. I am whole and healthy.

When I say my dreams and goals out loud, it's like casting a magical spell, with sparkles, effervescent and all.

Wow, what an incredible world we live in!

My heart leads the way in everything I do.

I sleep peacefully under the glow of the moon. I am very, very relaxed.

I will rise anew tomorrow, amazing and full of life. I am grateful for my beautiful power.

I manifest everything I desire, because I'm worthy and full of love and light.

I feel the wonder and awe I have for my amazing life.

I'm riding on a purple-glowing magic carpet through the dark, star-filled sky, attracting my dreams and legendary life.

I am open to spontaneous opportunities that pop out of wispy clouds in the night sky.

I am a child of the Universe, and the Universe conspires to help me manifest all of my amazing dreams and goals.

I'm an intuitive manifester. It's fun tapping into my intuition for guidance.

My heart will lead the way. I can always count on it to guide me in the right direction.

I will have the most magical and peaceful sleep tonight, like royalty in a kingdom of love.

Pillow Self-Talk Mantra

Choose one of the following. (See instructions, Chapter 5.)

- *I love my magical life.*
- *My mind is filled with awe.*
- *My dreams will bring answers tonight.*

SCRIPT: ALL IS WELL

Don't ask yourself at the end of the day if you did everything right. Ask yourself how well you loved, and then grow from your answer.

— L.R. KNOST

One of my favorite lines of self-talk is simply,

All is well.

So basic.

So fundamental.

Like whole milk, or home-cooked meals.

Or like the feeling you have when you know the flowers will blossom every spring. It's just, well... *matter of fact*. And in truth, it's always like this. Life is. Life is always... *All is well.* Everything works out in the end. Good perseveres. Comfy, cozy goodness.

It doesn't matter what is going on in the world. It doesn't matter what is going on in your life. No matter what is going on in this very moment for you, when you think the words, *All is well,* and you allow them to soothe and comfort you like a warm cup of cocoa, you will simply feel, indeed, that all is well.

Why is this important? Because when *All is well* is your focus, you can move forward and draw your dreams closer to you. You relax. You find forgiveness. You have a calmer demeanor. The corners of your mouth turn up. You have a knowing, a twinkling gleam in your eye.

Because you know... *All is well.*

Pillow Self-Talk Script: All Is Well

All is well.

Of course, all is well.

It always is.

I make room for magic.

I am love, and all is well.

The sun rises, and the sun sets, and all is well.

I look at the world around me tonight and feel bright and healthy, star-bright energy—a night full of optimism and compassion. Joy is all around. All is well.

The leaves are born in the spring. The leaves shade me in the summer. The leaves gently fall in the autumn. The leaves recycle into the earth in the winter. The cycle of life is beautiful, and all is well.

I am the master of my mind. I sparkle like a starlit sky. I can feel it right now.

In the silent hour of the night, I am in harmony with the universe.

Through all the many phases of the moon, timeless and eternal... all is well.

The stars are there no matter, night or day, and all is well.

I am healthy and full of vitality. I am ready to rest tonight, and I welcome my dreams.

I am relaxed. All is well.

My imagination, aroused to shimmering excitement, brings my dreams to me.

I am an amazing person because I am kind, thoughtful, and patient.

The world is blessed, and I am blessed. We are all blessed.

My to-do list is a breeze, and all is well.

I have an unlimited supply of brilliant ideas, creativity, and sparkling love.

I was born knowing my way with my glittering truth. I reconnect with myself now.

My oh my, how sparkly life is! A marvelous life opens its arms to me. I walk into its arms, and all is well.

I'm excited to see what's next for my life, what's in store, and all the good that's coming my way.

Life is great, and all is well.

At the core of my soul is where my dreams blossom and glow.

My story is bliss. My story is life. My story is epic, everlasting, and it sings me to sleep like a lullaby.

Deep breath, now. Eyes relaxed.

Sweet dreams to me, because, always... all is well.

Pillow Self-Talk Mantra

Choose one of the following. (See instructions, Chapter 5.)

- *All is well.*
- *My life is great, and all is well.*
- *I am healthy, happy, and all is well.*

SCRIPT: WE ARE ONE

It was dark, now, the gossamer moon hanging among diamond stars in the soft black of the night.

— AMBER NEWBERRY

I talk all the time about the importance of thinking and feeling to make your dreams come true. One of the best ways to explore those elevated emotions that are so important to this process is to embrace a life in which you're in love with the *unity of the world.*

When you're wide open to the world, it can be a *wonderful place.*

Community and friends. Family and neighbors. Strangers, too. We are all made of the same stardust. We are all one. We are all connected, me to you, and you to me. And to everybody else, from the person standing next to you at the post office, to a child playing with her dog on the other side of the world, while you drift to sleep on your own soft pillow. *We are all connected.* Isn't that the most beautiful thought? This connection brings support, and this support brings health, synergy, and life.

All of this makes a better world and a better life for you.

Even as I dictate these words while I'm walking in Italy, I can't help but feel, deep down, this sense that *we are all connected*. I am imagining you reading this, once the book is in your hands, and I am connecting to you across time. It fills me with a magical sense of wonder and energy.

I want a world for myself, for my family, and especially for my daughter, where the people in her life are filled with optimism, creativity, awe, happiness, and generosity... therefore, helping one another, and making the world more peaceful. After all, great social movements begin in the minds of just a few courageous people. It starts with me. It starts with you.

Pillow Self-Talk Script: We Are One

We are one, and it is a beautiful feeling.

I am one with the people around me and in my life. The universe and I are one, and this connection supports me, and it feels beautiful.

I see you, and you see me. I feel you, and you feel me.

When I allow others to live their own truth, the whole world brightens like a full moon, guiding us through the night.

As twilight fills my soul with the richness of the night, I connect with the universe, and I can feel it... the universe has my back.

Being one with the world brings peace and joy to all.

I love life, and life loves me.

My night and dreams are full of opportunities, because I am always open to them.

I am worthy. We are all worthy.

Plants, animals, and all life... everything holds a special meaning in the universe.

Prosperity abounds with oneness.

I am excited to fall asleep tonight and meet new people in my dreams.

I love people.

I am passionate about learning from others, and it makes me so much smarter and wiser when I keep an open mind.

Whatever the question, love is the answer.

My life expands when I learn about other cultures, and I love learning about new ways to live.

I get phenomenal deep sleep, and I will do that tonight.

Connecting with others brings more light into my life.

Animals are fascinating, and they never cease to fill me with awe.

People can save people, and this fills me with love.

I am open-minded, magical, and living on the edge of beyond.

I look out across the sea of my mind, feeling waves of connection to people all over the world tonight.

The rainbows of cultures around the world make for the most beautiful tapestry, which I wrap myself in, as I drift off to sleep tonight.

We are all made from the same stardust. I love my life.

I am grateful to have the potential for such powerful connections with other human beings, and all living things.

When I open my heart to others, my whole world expands with sparkling, robust possibility. There is power in this connection.

I love helping others. It brightens my soul, making me a moonbeam in the night.

I welcome the opportunity to simply chat with strangers as I go about my day. I never know what magic will happen.

What a magnificent time to be alive! I am grateful for my beating heart.

Pillow Self-Talk Mantra

Choose one of the following. (See instructions, Chapter 5.)

- *We are one in this great life.*
- *I love the Universe.*
- *I open my heart to everyone.*

SCRIPT: THE GREAT, SPARKLING GALAXY

At night, I have wings.

— FRANZ RICHTER

Circumstances come, and circumstances go. Life ebbs, and life flows.

And through it all, you are simply a person on a big planet, spinning along in the great, sparkling galaxy. There's a great big existence out there, and when you step back to ponder this idea, a bit of tranquility soothes your nerves, like dusk settling into night. We're all interwoven threads in this giant tapestry of infinite existence.

One of my favorite things to do is to go outside and look at the stars on a dark night. Yowza... the in-your-face epic-ness of it, the grandeur, it's all so spectacular, that *whatever* is going on in my life... it just puts everything into perspective and soothes my soul.

If there's anything troubling you, whatever's going on in your life, if you're looking for answers to questions, then step outside to see the stars. Be amazed at the sight above. BJ Miller of Zenhospice.org says the following about this "star therapy," of looking at stars and finding awe and comfort in them:

> You realize that the light hitting your eye is ancient. Some of the stars that you're seeing, they no longer exist by the time the light gets to you. Just mulling the bare-naked facts of the cosmos is enough to thrill me, awe me, freak me out, and put all my neurotic anxieties in their proper place.

And remember... you have permission to think epically, and to feel magical, and brilliant, and amazing, *no matter the circumstances.* No matter what's going on, you get to choose your own response. That is perhaps your greatest power in life.

Pillow Self-Talk Script: The Great, Sparkling Galaxy

I am born from stars, and I live like a star.

I love tonight, because I am in charge of my life. I make it what I want. I am powerful, and I am relaxed.

I attract beautiful things.

No matter what is happening, I am in a great big world full of wonder and opportunity.

I am falling asleep with generous thoughts, expansive ideas, and a heart full of awe and mystery.

I go on the most incredible sleep adventures every night.

I breathe in the unknown and come alive. Out of the shadows and into the dazzling starlight.

Peace relaxes me into a deep sleep. No worries, no little things to sweat, because life is so much bigger, so much more.

I am grateful for my attitude and seeing the silver linings in life.

My destiny is being fulfilled in wondrous and exciting ways. The stars above shine down on me as I sleep tonight.

I take a deep breath and breathe in relaxation. I am ready for the most amazing sleep.

Everything is working out for me as I dream tonight.

There is always more than enough for me, overflowing love, peace, and abundance.

I slow down, I unbend, I uncoil, I relax into the night, and a soft blanket of calm puts me to sleep.

I am a human, lying down to sleep, on a planet spinning around in a great big, beautiful galaxy.

I am ready for sleep. It's coming to take me into dreamland, where wishes twinkle, and inspiration sparkles.

I love my life, and my life loves me.

I am worthy.

Pillow Self-Talk Mantra

Choose one of the following. (See instructions, Chapter 5.)

- *I am filled with the awe of Life.*
- *The stars guide my dreams tonight.*
- *I am getting deep, peaceful sleep tonight.*

LUMINOUS HEALTH, HEALING & LONGEVITY

Here's the thing... it's fine and dandy to want to attract wealth, and success, and love. But if you don't have your health, then all of that is meaningless. But when your health is magnificent, shining, brilliant, and strong, then it lifts up every other part of your life. Career success is easier because you have the energy to act on ideas. Relationships are better because you have more energy to give to others.

Everything improves with health. Your health is therefore not only important as its own end, but also as an important focus for manifesting everything else in the dream life you seek. The focus can be for general health, well-being, and longevity. It can also be for healing a specific ailment, injury, or disease.

Lissa Rankin, M.D., author of *Mind Over Medicine*, explains the importance of our mindset when healing our bodies from disease, because your thoughts can change your biochemistry. What your brain expects to happen in the future affects your physiological state. For this reason, our thoughts hold incredible medicine, and when we're relaxed and rested, the body can begin to work on repairing itself.

If small things keep happening that impact your health—whether it's a recurring headache, you twist your ankle, or the flu hits—first things first. Don't get bummed. Don't get down on yourself. It doesn't mean you're doing anything wrong. But it might mean you should take a look at your lifestyle and see if perhaps you could use better sleep, or some self-care. Maybe you need to rearrange your schedule to give you more "me" time.

Yeah... maybe you just need a day off. Or a year.

Look at the frequency and vibe you're giving off. Are you operating at peak sparkle? If not, then focus on love, sweet love. Love yourself back to robust health.

Sometimes it's helpful to consider the "practical" (or *material*) things, like vitamins, diet, meditation, and exercise. Life is a dance between the practical and the "magical" (energy). Everything is matter and energy. I believe energy trumps it all, but that doesn't mean I don't pay attention to the practical elements as well. (A topic for another time!)

Let's start with Pillow Self-Talk, because it all begins with self-talk. It's the first place I recommend starting when you want to improve health, or glow brighter than ever.

This section includes the following Pillow Self-Talk scripts for *Luminous Health, Healing, and Longevity*:

- *Glowing Health*
- *Fun Fitness*
- *Lasting Longevity*
- *Heroic Healing*

SCRIPT: GLOWING HEALTH

Life is a balance between rest and movement.

— RAJNEESH

When you have your health, you have the energy to manifest your dreams. When you feel good, it's easier to get things done. A healthy person is usually in a happier mood. And sleep is integral to good health. So is your self-talk. We're going to combine these ideas.

Use your self-talk to inspire your focus on good health. Use it to elevate your relaxed feelings to attract and manifest good health. This is where healing can take place, in a relaxed body. Then, you'll use your self-talk to get an amazing night's sleep, too. Feel free to add some specifics, such as certain body parts you want to focus on, like your eyes, or teeth, or your knee that's been wanting some love, or any other body parts.

You can also use a script like this and add specific lines to prepare your body if you're going to have any sort of medical procedure. If there's something you're going to do that you're nervous about, then you can fill your heart and mind with glowing self-talk, telling yourself how much you're looking forward to the procedure, being happy about it, knowing with confidence how every hand that touches you is a healing hand, and how great it's going to go.

If you need to take medication, and you're concerned about side effects, it makes sense to think positively about the medicine and about all the benefits it will have for you. You can fill your brain with powerful thoughts about *how amazing the drug is for you, how lucky you are to live in a time with modern medicine, and how it's going to be wonderful.* Believe in what you're doing, and starting with your words is the way to go.

And most of all, no matter what you're considering, don't operate from a place of fear. Whether you decide to do any medical intervention or not, you want to have the best, strongest mindset to support *your* decision. Our minds are incredibly powerful, and the placebo effect is real. Take full advantage of this. I do all the time.

Sweet dreams, my friend.

Pillow Self-Talk Script: Glowing Health

I am healthy. I love being healthy, and it makes my life extra amazing.

I shimmer and shine, and I glow with health.

My immune system is tough as nails, and my mind is crystal clear.

I am worthy of being healthy, and I like making healthy choices for my body.

I love being healthy, and being healthy loves me.

I have a beautiful body. I love my body. I love it so much!

I enjoy healthy meals made with love.

My skin is young, and radiant, and smooth, and glowing.

I am relaxed, so very, very relaxed.

I am healthy from head to toe, inside and out. My cells buzz with energy. It is natural for my body to be healthy and full of vibrancy.

I'm able to get everything I want done, every day. I also get a full night's rest and sleep.

I love life. I love my life. I love me!

Life is full of opportunities everywhere I turn, and being healthy means I am primed and ready for anything.

I am whole, worthy, healthy, and happy.

I have confidence in my brain and body. My hormones are in tip-top shape.

Thank you, Life, for tonight. My mind is calm.

I love you, legs. I love you, back. I love you, face. I love you, feet. I love you, body. I love you so very, very much.

Being healthy means attaining my dreams and goals faster.

I love making healthy choices about food and exercise. I love getting amazing sleep, and I'll be doing that tonight.

I love taking care of my health, and I am completely relaxed about it.

Peace, love, and light comfort me, and I know that abundant health is mine.

I'm living my best life, and I get to go to sleep with delight filling my heart.

My teeth and gums are beautiful and healthy. My eyes are extraordinarily powerful.

I feel the loving space around my body, and it's filled with healthy energy that will comfort me as I sleep.

I attract luminous health.

I am grateful for my healthy body. I am generous with compliments for my beautiful body, because I'm worth it.

I am greatness, and I can attain all of my health goals. Tonight, I fall asleep knowing that my peaceful energy draws my health goals to me faster.

I will awaken refreshed and ready to take on the day, full of health and vigor.

I am ready for sleep now. I'm relaxed and content, calm and tranquil.

I'm taking a nice, soft, and deep breath.

Good night.

Pillow Self-Talk Mantra

Choose one of the following. (See instructions, Chapter 5.)

- *I have a strong body.*
- *I have a radiant, healthy body.*
- *I am getting the best deep sleep tonight.*

SCRIPT: FUN FITNESS

Think in the morning. Act in the noon. Eat in the evening. Sleep in the night.

— WILLIAM BLAKE

This Pillow Self-Talk script is for people who want to be more fit, or for people who are passionate about fitness in general. The script contains lines about movement, and exercise, and being inspired to do those things, even if you currently aren't.

When you are more fit, you'll feel magnitudes better. You will feel stronger, both physically *and* mentally. And this will empower you, because it boosts your confidence and self-esteem. Physical activity also improves sleep, especially deep sleep.

Fitness is cool in that it's a choice you make and can take action with immediately. As a result, you feel some of the effects right away, which does wonders for your confidence. You took control, you took action, you moved your body, and this is empowering.

One of the most important steps in attaining fitness goals is to start by loving yourself as you are *now*. It doesn't matter if you can walk one block or ten. It doesn't matter if you can do one pushup or twenty.

Love yourself, now. As you are.

When you do, your transformation will happen *waaay* more easily—and much faster. Loving yourself *the way you are* makes all the difference in the world. Trust me... when we love ourselves as we are, *we feel more worthy of improving,* and we therefore start taking more focused and serious steps toward the things we want, in order to attain the goals we set.

Plus? We have less stress in our bodies when we love ourselves. This means less inflammation, less pain. When there's less inflammation, you feel better. And when you feel better, you have more energy to pursue your fitness goals.

Fitness comes in many shapes and sizes, so you can approach it in different ways. You can set intentions for getting to the gym, or to do more things socially that include moving your body. Bowling anyone? Pickle ball? Dancing?

When my family was self-isolating in our little apartment in Italy during COVID-19, we bought a portable ping-pong net that fits on any table. We put it in our cute, tiny Italian kitchen, right on the table. We played every day, sometimes for hours! What a great way to get more movement without even having to leave the house. And it never even felt like exercise. It was just... *playing!*

There are a variety of lines in the following script to address several different situations, so you'll want to figure out where you are with your fitness goals and focus on the most relevant lines. You might also want to add a few custom lines that are tailored to your specific dreams and goals.

Being specific is very helpful for this type of Pillow Self-Talk. For instance, if you want to increase your bench-press by a certain amount, write a line of self-talk that has the exact number in it. If you want to weigh a certain amount, or reduce your waist to a certain size, then state the actual numbers, and consider using this for your Pillow Self-Talk Mantra.

Pillow Self-Talk Script: Fun Fitness

I love being fit. My body feels tight and powerful.

I love my life, and I shower myself with great fitness thoughts.

My fit body is strong, and I move effortlessly like a supple leopard.

Moving my body feels amazing, and it gives me energy.

I choose healthy living, because it's good for me, and I love me.

My body loves feeling strong and flexible. I am strong and flexible.

I love my beautiful shape.

I love moving, stretching, and strengthening my body every day.

I have the energy to pursue my fitness goals. My body is strong and capable.

I am grateful for my fitness.

I am having a beautiful night tonight. I smile with joy, and I am excited about everything that is happening in my life.

Exercise is one of my favorite things to do, because it feels so good.

I have great time-management habits, and I always make time to exercise.

I wake up every day with a radiant fitness mindset. I love moving my body and feeling my strength in every step. It's easy getting up from sitting. It's easy bending down to touch my toes.

I'm fit, strong, and sexy. I glide when I move.

I am worthy of taking time in my day to move my body.

Thank you for my super strong back.

Fitness and exercise help make my dreams come true, because they inspire my health and motivation.

I have a galaxy's worth of peace and calm in me right now.

Getting deep, restful sleep is a great way to build muscle and strength.

My body reflects my internal state, thoughts, and feelings.

I love walking, and I know it's super for my brain and body. I think creative ideas on my walks, and every step gives me more inspiration.

My heart always leads the way. It's healthy and strong.

I am grateful for my super fit body, with my sexy shape and all. I am a goddess/god.

I am excited to wake up tomorrow and exercise. I'm the master conductor of my fit life.

I stand in my own power. My body feels nice and tight. I am strong and healthy. Good night, good night.

Pillow Self-Talk Mantra

Choose one of the following. (See instructions, Chapter 5.)

- *I am strong and fit.*
- *I love moving my body.*
- *My body is amazing.*

SCRIPT: LASTING LONGEVITY

I'm chasing my dreams straight to the top, into a sky that has no limits.

— PETER HANDKE

It's easy to embrace the mindset of living past 120 years when you realize that some people already live that long. So when I think of the future, and when I ponder longevity, *I go big*. I factor in future technological advancements, and I aim high, up to 180 youthful years, just like the biohacker and longevity expert Dave Asprey.

Why not? There's something mystical that happens when you *think big* and go gargantuan with your dreams and goals. Maybe it's the notion that, "if you shoot for the moon and miss, you'll still land among the stars." Meaning, maybe I shoot for 180 and land at 145. I'll take it! With the future, anything is possible. Who knows what fancy new technologies will spring up—bioinformatics, genomics, custom medicine, gene replacement therapies, mitochondrial repair, and things we haven't dreamed up yet—all allowing for wildly increased lifespan. That's why I'm so optimistic about it!

And you know what else? There's something fascinating about the sparkling mindset that follows that bold claim of living to 180... it actually *relaxes* me! Why? Because any fear or stress about illnesses, real or imagined, they don't have a home in this mindset because, "Sorry, illness, you're not in my reality. I'm living to 180!"

What else does this bold claim do? It expands all kinds of other possibilities in my life. Such as creating an abundance of time and energy to do everything I want, because it'll be a long time before I turn 180!

Pillow Self-Talk Script: Lasting Longevity

I am living a long, blissful life, because I take great care of myself.

My body hums with life, and I feel young and vibrant.

I am calm and relaxed, which creates peace in my body, allowing it to heal and protect me.

I cherish my health, and I take care of myself in all ways, which will ensure I live a long, healthy life, to the beautiful age of 180 or beyond.

My body is designed for longevity. No matter what my age, my eyes sparkle, filled with childlike wonder.

I have incredible health, and I'm going to live a very long time.

I'm going to live past 180 years. I am excited about the technology being developed right now to support this.

I am worthy to receive everything in the dream life that I design.

I create time and space for health, and for living my beautiful life. I am grateful.

I love being a kind and generous person.

I bless everything in my life right now. My heart, my brain, my soul, my home, my bed, my pillow.

I believe in me. I believe in my body. I believe in my longevity. I believe in my healthy genes.

I breathe easily and give my body and mind the rest I deserve.

I am worthy of longevity.

I have a powerful brain and memory. I remember everything. Words come to me easily. My recall is effortless.

I make choices that are deeply loving to my life. I relax tonight into the clarity of my mind.

I. Am. Amazing. I easily align myself with health and longevity.

I am kind, thoughtful, and I love imagining myself living in the future, decades from now.

My back, and neck, and legs all feel great. I see myself running on the beach, skiing when I'm a hundred, and gliding easily through life.

I am grateful that my youthful genes are expressed during my deep, beautiful sleep.

I am open to wellness, and my genes dazzle with vibrant health. I relax with a smile, thinking this, feeling this, and knowing this.

I'm calm, relaxed, and this longevity mindset is helping me to live a very long, happy life.

Pillow Self-Talk Mantra

Choose one of the following. (See instructions, Chapter 5.)

- *I am living past 180 years.*
- *I feel young and healthy.*
- *My longevity genes are expressing right now.*

SCRIPT: HEROIC HEALING

I have made a pact with the night, I have felt it softly healing me.

— AIMÉ CÉSAIRE

The human body is an incredible thing. Miraculous and magical. And capable. So very capable. There's massive potential and opportunity for healing. It happens. People have spontaneous healings all the time. The words you hold in your mind express themselves through the body. Are you thinking elevated and uplifted words? Let's do that tonight!

If you're healing from something right now, whether it's a serious illness, or a cold or flu, or headache, or a broken bone, or a strained muscle... this script applies to you.

What does this script do?

It brings you peace and confidence and a relaxed mindset.

What does that do?

Reduces stress.

Why is that important?

Stress creates inflammation, and inflammation creates pain and disease.

Heroic Healing Pillow Self-Talk is designed to help you think amazing thoughts and feel positive feelings. This is part of the recipe for manifesting, which you know by now. And you need to do this no matter what's going on inside or outside of you right now.

You want to think and feel *whole and healthy* despite the conditions of your life today. To bring healing into your life, think and feel healed and whole, right now. It can seem tricky at first. Like, feeling whole, in the middle of a pounding headache? Is that even possible? Yes, it is. That's your goal as you rest and ease into sleep.

One way is to simply focus your heart on love. Think about something you love. I use the Pillow Self-Talk Mantra for this, too. If I have a headache, I go through the thinking, saying, and mouthing, "I love my bed" (or daughter, or the stars, or the rejuvenation that a good sleep brings). I think of something I love, and then love becomes my focus. Or I keep repeating that I feel great, even if I don't. I just keep saying it anyway.

A few years ago, I had a cold, and I kept repeating to myself how great I felt, over and over in my head, while I relaxed and binge-watched *Grey's Anatomy*. Every time I took a sip of my hot coffee or tea, I imagined it soothing my throat and healing my body. Every night, I went to sleep, confident I'd wake up the next day feeling better.

Did it work? Did I shorten the duration of my illness?

I feel like it did. I guess I'll never truly know, but here is what I do know: It was a hell of a lot more enjoyable having a positive mindset during that time than to have a negative, defeatist attitude. So there's that.

Ok, secretly, just between you and me?... Deep down, *I know it helped*... and guess what?

The stronger the belief, the faster the healing. Having a deep, rooted knowing that your body is designed to heal is *the key to the speed*. In fact, according to Dr. Joe Dispenza,

> *"After years of interviewing people who experienced spontaneous remission, I realized they all believed that a higher intelligence lived within them. This inner power was giving them life, and it knew more than they, as humans, could ever know. The power that made the body can heal the body."*

The point is to change your focus to one that is uplifted, and believe in the process. Believe in you. Believe in your body's ability to heal itself. It might take practice to get there, and that's ok. Write yourself your own *prescription of self-love*. And keep doing the glorious work of thinking and feeling elevated thoughts and emotions, and use your Pillow Self-Talk to help you get there.

Another way to do this is to think *of the future you,* who is already healed and healthy. Step into that person, right here and right now, and imagine what that would feel like to feel healthy and whole. How would your body change? What would you do?

You can approach this mindset through gratitude, too. For example, if you have a sore back, then you can imagine, think, and feel how grateful you are for your healed back. Acting *as if it's already healed*. It would feel amazing, right? So imagine that.

The lines in tonight's Pillow Self-Talk will help you do that, but it's also about thinking and feeling things that go beyond a specific body part or specific disease. You want to enter a *general mindset* that is one of *abundance and relaxation.*

Pillow Self-Talk Script: Heroic Healing

I am healed. I am healthy. I feel good. I am whole.

I have the most amazing dreams, full of vivid colors and textures.

My body loves to heal. I feel love with my heart, moment by moment.

I am here to thrive. I was born to thrive. It is my destiny.

I feel a current within, as I begin to draw my dreams closer to me. I am grateful for my healing.

When I change my thoughts, I change my feelings. This changes my biochemistry. This is how I heal myself.

I deserve to live a healthy life. I am whole.

I am overflowing with gratitude and awash with love for myself.

I relax right now, because I am healing right now, as I speak. My body's innate intelligence knows exactly what to do. I close my eyes and rest while it does the work for me.

My heart expands with love, and we are all one.

I let go of all fear, right now. I'm taking responsibility for my success and health. Now, and for the rest of my long life.

I am blessed with perfect health. My heart will lead the way.

I think and feel wholeness, because my thoughts are the perfect medicine.

I take a deep breath, because it's a beautiful night for healing.

My body is amazing and is capable of healing itself. The human body is awesome. Magnificent.

Healing energy is all around me, and my body is worthy of love.

Everyone who touches me spreads healing energy through me.

I am a rapid healer, and it is my birthright to feel healthy.

I breathe easy. I breathe so very, very easy. Tonight is all that matters. Deep relaxing breath.

Forgiveness and forgiving are easy for me. I am whole and healthy.

I can expect my body to heal, because it's a self-healing superstar.

I love my body so much. I feel easy, relaxed, and star-bright. I shine with confidence and radiate healing in every cell of my body. I glow with healing all through the night while I sleep. I am love. I am love. I am so much love.

Thank you for my healed body.

I rest easy and fall asleep with peaceful thoughts, waking with freshness in my body. I feel great!

I have courage, and I have faith in my magical body to heal itself.

My cells and hormones are healing and healthy. I love them, and they love me.

I close my eyes and rest easy tonight with splendid, peaceful, and healthy thoughts.

Pillow Self-Talk Mantra

Choose one of the following. (See instructions, Chapter 5.)

- *I am relaxed and filled with peace.*
- *I love my life. I love healing.*
- *I am healed. I am healthy.*

CELESTIAL SURRENDER & PEACE

This section is all about surrender and finding your deepest calm. It can be surrendering troubles and fears to lighten your load. It can be letting go with ease and learning to live with less attachment to things.

Here's one thing I know: *There's something better when I surrender.* I live a life in which I dance with the Universe—it's where I surrender. I might be in the captain's seat of my rocket ship into the deep space of my life, but the Universe is my co-pilot. It helps in ways I've known and ways I never would've guessed. Always good, always making me a winner in the end.

Enjoy this section, and allow it to help bring you to the deepest peace you've ever known.

As always, sweet dreams.

This section includes the following Pillow Self-Talk scripts for *Celestial Surrender & Calm*:

- *Forgiveness for Freedom*
- *I Let Go with Ease*
- *Silencing Stress*
- *Addressing Anxiety & Fear*
- *Adios, Addictions & Cravings*
- *Coping with Grief*
- *Profound Peace*

SCRIPT: FORGIVENESS FOR FREEDOM

I have drunk the night
and swallowed the stars.
I am dancing with abandon
and singing with rapture.
There is not a thing I do not love.
There is not a person I have not forgiven.
I feel a universe of love.
I feel a universe of light.

— KAMAND KOJOURI

Forgiveness is one of the most important elements to living a magical life. It's so important that I want to write it again:

Forgiveness is one of the most important elements to living a magical life.

Forgiveness.

Forgiveness.

Forgiveness.

That is simply because, when you forgive, you release dark emotions that would only put the brakes on your dreams.

When you forgive, you liberate your spirit. Forgiveness frees your soul. It absolutely makes you shine brighter than ever.

Which helps you manifest your dreams faster, because abundance comes easier. You have more space in your heart for more loving energies, and more space in your brain for creativity and taking action toward your legendary life. When you use forgiveness to release a dark emotion, a cloud of related thoughts that were activated by that feeling disappear, like fog burning off in the morning sunshine.

Forgiveness comes in two flavors:

1. Forgiving yourself
2. Forgiving others

A lot of people walk through life feeling guilty for things in their past, their mistakes or failures. The good news is that, as your self-talk continues to improve, and you attract more love and peace as a result, you'll find it easier to forgive yourself and others.

You will learn to look at the past as leveling-up your life lessons, even if some of them were painful at the time. It gives you wisdom and courage, and the knowledge to move forward with the winds of freedom at your back.

When it comes to forgiving other people, it's a necessity to living your dream life. It just is. So think of your ability to forgive—which is to say, *to let go*—consider it one of your superpowers. This doesn't mean you don't have boundaries. It means you let go and move on.

And remember, the more you *love yourself* and the more worthiness you feel inside your own heart *for yourself,* the easier you'll find it to forgive other people. It's a natural result.

Often times, people struggle with forgiving other people because they don't even forgive themselves for things. But once you start forgiving yourself, you'll find that you have the knowledge, love, and courage to forgive others.

Tonight's Pillow Self-Talk is written to encourage all forms of forgiveness. And with this forgiveness, you also get inner peace, which leads to the *very best sleep.*

Pillow Self-Talk Script: Forgiveness for Freedom

Tonight, as I move into my slow dance with the universe, sleep comes to me, and I am full of forgiveness.

My elegant life expands with forgiveness, and I'm grateful for my power to forgive.

I forgive myself for the mistakes I have made. I learn from them, and I move on. They have made me a wiser person.

I always strive to be the best person I can be.

Only greatness lies before me. I am ready.

All is well, and we are all one, and I am so utterly grateful for forgiveness.

I forgive those who have wronged me. I release my negative feelings, and I look forward to my brilliant, magical, exciting future.

I'm living a new life, of my own design, and it feels good to be in charge of my feelings.

I think good thoughts, and I feel good feelings, because those are the ingredients to drawing my brilliant dreams to me tonight.

Forgiving others is one of my superpowers.

My life transforms when I forgive. It's perfect, it's ripe, and it makes life juicy and bright.

Forgiveness is freedom. Forgiveness is happiness. Forgiveness is wholeness, and I feel immediate relief in my chest and heart when I forgive.

I'm living the most amazing life, and it's filled with awe. Thank you, Life. Thank you, Me.

I release, I forgive, I love, and I am doing the right thing. Forgiveness is always the right thing.

My heart expands with strength and courage whenever I forgive.

I use my time wisely and make the most of my life.

I shimmer and shine. I'm open. I'm divine.

Forgiving feels good, because I like moving on. It's smart. It's wise. It's healing. It's love.

I am worthy of forgiveness. We are all worthy of forgiveness.

The time is now for love and light all through the night. I am love. I am light. I am a dazzling delight.

I am so blessed, because I know how to forgive.

I love how I think. I love how I feel. I love the power I have to get the best sleep ever.

Forgiveness is fun. Forgiveness is fabulous fun.

I surrender into a deep sleep, relaxed and peaceful, and waves of forgiveness wash over me.

My life is full of love, and I step through the world looking for ways to show this.

I am so lucky, because I am bursting with forgiveness. Thank you, forgiveness, for being possible.

I sleep peacefully, resting and relaxing my body as it sinks into my comfortable bed.

At the core of my soul is where my dreams glow. I am awash with excitement and love, and I will wake up tomorrow, ready for an amazing day.

I love forgiveness, and forgiveness loves me.

Pillow Self-Talk Mantra

Choose one of the following. (See instructions, Chapter 5.)

- *Forgiving gives me peace.*
- *I love forgiveness. It opens my heart.*
- *I always forgive myself and others.*

SCRIPT: I LET GO WITH EASE

When I let go of who I am,

I become what I might be.

— Lao Tzu

Letting go means taking a close look at your ego, as well as the attachments you have to things in life.

The ego has its place... it helps keep you alive, and it can be helpful when it comes to self-love, such as creating boundaries in your life, and making you feel worthy enough to prioritize your own needs. But sometimes, the ego gets bruised. At times like this, letting go and relaxing the ego can help your well-being and give you a sense of peace. When this happens, you feel better.

And when you feel better, you live better. You attract better.

If something is weighing on your mind tonight because something happened earlier that's bothering you, *just let it go.* Make the actual, physical gesture of opening your hands and symbolically releasing it. Ask yourself, will this matter a year from now? In almost all cases, it won't. And once you see that, you'll feel a shift inside your core to a place of peace.

Pillow Self-Talk Script: I Let Go with Ease

I focus on things that matter. I let go of anything that doesn't serve me.

Release and relief, that's what I'm doing right now.

I let it go. I let it all go. The deeper I breathe, the deeper I go.

I am calm. I am confident. I am self-assured. I am worthy of all my heart's desires. I have fun letting go.

I celebrate letting go as I move upward and onward in my journey.

I open my hands and take a deep breath as I let go. I cherish the lessons I have learned.

I let go with ease, and I easily attract the best things.

I think differently. I make different choices. I have crossed the river of change, and there's no going back.

Possibilities are around every corner, behind every star in the sky.

When I let go, I immediately feel better.

I welcome gratitude and love into my life.

I freely give up my old identity, and I leave it behind like dust in the wind. I'm living a completely new, magically brilliant life of my design.

I am thankful to wake up in my bed every day.

I am dazzled by my own abilities and competence. I let go with ease, and I feel total peace, calm, and equanimity.

Everything always works out for me. My mind is mastered.

My muscles are supple and relaxed. I'm ready for my deep sleep.

The doors between dimensions open for me tonight, so that I may experience the mystical in my dream sleep. Synchronicities are swirling around in my life all the time.

I have broken the chains of my past. Nothing holds me down. I rise and rise every day. I rise full of love, confidence, and extraordinary knowing. I am here. I am transformed.

The day is over, and that means it is in the past. I am not attached to it. I learned from my life, and I move on with sweet, gentle grace.

My arms are open, to receive all the opportunities coming to me in my dreams tonight.

I am eternally grateful for all that is good in the world.

Good night, sweet love, good night.

Pillow Self-Talk Mantra

Choose one of the following. (See instructions, Chapter 5.)

- *I let go with ease.*
- *I breathe deeply. I'm filled with peace.*
- *Synchronicities are swirling all around me.*

SCRIPT: SILENCING STRESS

And the night shall be filled with music,

And the cares that infest the day,

Shall fold their tents,

and silently steal away.

— HENRY WADSWORTH LONGFELLOW

When you live a magical life, like you will with your new positive mindset, stress is just not a big thing anymore. That's because you learn how to navigate life by finding the silver linings, seeing the opportunities, and thriving. You default to a mindset of seeing possibilities, learning lessons, and taking on new challenges with verve and gusto.

If a stressful event shows up, no biggie, you've got powerful skills for working through it.

If there is something stressing you out, take a moment to remind yourself that *this too shall pass*. As Tony Robbins says,

"Life happens *for us*, not *to us*."

See yourself on the other side of the stress. Focus on the good things in life. Tap into gratitude. There are many ways to process a stressful event, and you don't *ever* have to let it dim your shine. Learn from it, and move on.

You are amazing. You are incredible. Feel the love of knowing that.

Pillow Self-Talk Script: Silencing Stress

I honor my journey, and I weave my own tapestry for living life. I am magnificent.

My brain rests easy, day and night.

I solve problems when I sleep, and I find creative solutions in my dreams.

I slip easily into sleep.

It's time to rest now, after a life well-lived today.

Relaxation is a key to manifestation.

Superb and glorious, unconditional love surrounds me tonight, wrapping me tight like a blanket. All is wonderfully well.

I reclaim my star-bright shine. Life, joy, and love.

The silence of the night hugs me and comforts me in a warm, soothing embrace.

Awe, gratitude, and peace wash over me, through me, and all around me, tonight.

I don't have to know all the details of how my goals will manifest. My dreams work on that when I go to sleep at night.

The awesomeness of life glitters and sprinkles around me, like a million twinkling stars.

My body is relaxed. My mind is calm. I am whole.

I'm always learning and growing, like a seed sprouting with potential.

My life gets more fabulous each and every day.

I support others with love and kindness.

Silver linings are sparkly and beautiful.

Ocean waves of peace are washing over me now. Ahhh, it feels so good.

I have legendary sleep, and it sets up tomorrow for every possible success.

Sleep and I have a great relationship. It makes me smile.

My heart leads the way in my life.

It's time for a quiet night of sleep and precious, sweet dreams full of life and love. I am ready. Good night to me.

Pillow Self-Talk Mantra

Choose one of the following. (See instructions, Chapter 5.)

- *My mind is calm.*
- *I am happy. I am so very, very happy.*
- *I slip easily into sleep.*

SCRIPT: ADDRESSING ANXIETY & FEAR

If you're depressed, you're living in the past.

If you're anxious, you're living in the future.

If you're at peace, you're living in the present.

— LAO TZU

The first time I heard this 2500-year-old quote from Lao Tzu, I was listening to a podcast, and I stopped in my tracks. *It made so much sense!* It was a light bulb moment. *Ding-ding!*

I immediately took each line and applied it to my life, trying it out. I could feel its truth surging through me.

Tonight, we'll dedicate our Pillow Self-Talk to dealing with anxiety. How true that anxiety and worries come from imagining bad things *in the future*. Things that have not happened yet. With positive self-talk, you simply wash away those fears. You replace them with thoughts and feelings of love.

And it works!

And the more you do it, the easier it gets, and the more effective the results. Pretty soon, you are unavailable for anxiety because you're filling your heart with feelings of love and living your legendary life.

It becomes the new you. Pure transformation, butterfly-style.

Anxiety is tension from worried thoughts. Fear operates from survival emotions. Both are uncomfortable, but both can be eliminated with love, because there's something fascinating about your brain: It can't feel those two opposing feelings at the same time. That's just the way the brain works.

Neat, huh? If you feel love, you can't feel fear.

Use that to your advantage.

So, if you feel anxious, change your thoughts to *anything about love*. Love of your partner, or dog, or bookstores, or chocolate, or a certain song. I repeat, if you feel fear, anxiety or unease, then flip the switch to love: flowers, springtime, friends, new horizons, exciting possibilities.

Gone are the days of tightness in your neck or chest. No more scrunched up foreheads. Tonight, starting now, you can welcome feelings of love and relaxation. This Pillow Self-Talk script is filled with words of soothing and empowering love. *Buh-bye*, anxiety.

Even better, you can train your brain to automatically switch to love mode (or any elevated emotion) anytime anxiety, fear, or worry knocks at your door. When this happens, you very simply answer the door with love.

Knock knock.

Who's there?

Anxiety and fear.

Go away, nothin' but Love here.

This little rhyming riddle might seem silly, and that's the point. It's great for all ages, and being light-hearted is the first step, not taking things too seriously. If you can remember to say this cute riddle, and let it serve as a reminder to always open up the door to love, then fewer and fewer things will give you anxiety. And after a while, you just respond to everything with love. It's walking around the world, stepping through life feeling bliss, feeling unencumbered. Feeling *light*.

Go boldly into your life, full of worthiness and love, because you are 100% worthy of peace and greatness.

Pillow Self-Talk Script: Addressing Anxiety & Fear

I am resourceful.

I am worthy and brave.

Tonight, I welcome: Appreciation. Worthiness. Wholeness. Self-Love. Smiles and winks to myself.

My neck and shoulders are relaxed. I am safe. I feel safe.

I inhale peace with every breath.

I breathe peace and relaxation. I liberate myself from anxiety and release it. I watch it drift, up, up, up and away from me.

My opinions are valued, because I'm honest and experienced.

I cultivate inner calm and relax into the night.

Resting heals me. I am whole.

I am strong, I thrive through anything, and the Universe has my back.

I am in charge of my thoughts and actions, and it feels amazing to have my needs met. Love heals me.

The unknown is part of my life, and I love it. It's exciting, and I thrive. I am open to how tomorrow wishes to unfold for me. I choose positivity.

Calm, soft waves on the shore of my mind soothe my thoughts.

I love and forgive myself, now and always.

I am in the right place, at the right time.

I release the need for approval from others from my life. My hands are relaxed. Deep breath.

I am loved deeply, and my healing energy spreads to others.

Anything is possible, and when I send out vibrations of love and energy for something, I'm telling the Universe, "Yes, more of this!"

Gratitude, I let it fill my soul. I feel the marvelous magic of it, as life expands when gratitude begins.

I rest easy, knowing the perfect solutions are already coming to me.

I appreciate... I appreciate... I appreciate. Everything.

Pillow Self-Talk Mantra

Choose one of the following. (See instructions, Chapter 5.)

- *I am free, and full of peace.*
- *I am resilient.*
- *I am smart, capable, and happy.*

SCRIPT: ADIOS, ADDICTIONS & CRAVINGS

Sunrise is the start of something beautiful: the day.

Sunset is the start of something beautiful: the night.

— JUANSEN DIZON

Self-talk is used extensively in cognitive therapy settings, and it can be helpful to free yourself from addiction and cravings. I'm not a doctor, and I don't pretend to be one, but whether you want to cut back on sugar, or cut out cigarettes, your positive self-talk can play a big role in reaching your goal.

When it comes to overcoming addictions and living a balanced life, *you are the answer.* Your mind is profoundly effective and capable. It's time to look deep inside your soul and see how worthy you are of living your best life. You are your greatest ally, because your thoughts are the most powerful tool in the universe for changing your actions. When you reprogram your mind with positive, uplifting self-talk, you boost your self-esteem, and you feel more worthy of achieving the thing you seek. When that happens, you make better choices in your life.

One of the important tips for helping you succeed with overcoming an addiction is loving yourself *now*, the way you are *today*. When you have self-love and self-worth, and you come from a place of loving yourself—*in this moment*—you set the foundation for much easier change, sometimes even effortless. You simply make better choices. It's as if your body wants to work *with you* because you love it.

In the following script, you want to take the specifics for the addiction you are releasing, and use those words in the script. The script includes some blank spots for you to fill in. For example, if you desire to consume less sugar, you could write this simple and powerful line:

I release the need for sugar.

If you say this line repeatedly as your Pillow Self-Talk mantra (see Chapter 5), you'll be amazed at the effect. Do this every night for sixteen nights, and see what happens. Do this throughout the day, too. No pressure or stress, just say those lines in your Pillow Self-Talk scripts and several times throughout the day. *Even while eating sugar.* Start now, speaking gently and lovingly as you say it. Watch what happens as you start making healthier choices, and the desire for sugar decreases.

Another way to think about it is like this... once you go through the "releasing" statement, then let it go, and don't focus on *resisting the thing*. Instead, focus on what you *want to attract*. Carl Jung said, *"What you resist persists."* In other words, if you're trying to release your addiction to sugar, go ahead and set the intention that you're releasing it with your self-talk, and feel good about it, and then fill your self-talk with things that you *do want*... like healthy choices, happiness, etc. What would that kind of *healthy living* look like? How would it feel? How happy would you be if you had that kind of life? What would you be doing? Imagine those things for your life, and your subconscious will work to make them real.

Pillow Self-Talk Script: Adios, Addictions & Cravings

I'm drifting across the night sky, relaxed and rested. It's easy to breathe, and I relax and ease into peace.

Thank you, Life, for today. I release _____ from my life forever.

Everything is always aligning for me in the best possible ways.

I release any and all addictions. And I am at peace about this.

I am in the right place, at the right time.

I am happy and making healthy choices for my life and my body.

Good-bye, _____.

I make healthy choices.

I feel love with all of my heart, moment by moment.

I love me, and I love my body.

I make wonderful, positive gains in my life when I release _____ from it.

I am patient, I am forgiving, and I am compassionate with myself.

My personal vision sets the course for my life.

My smart choices lead to a better life.

I am relaxed, and my dreams are filled with peace.

My body feels whole and healthy, in every cell, from head to toe. Inside and out. I feel young, and I am beautiful. I release and release, and I find peace.

_____ does nothing for me, and it doesn't have a place in my glowing, healthy life.

I love and forgive myself completely. I deserve all the wonderful, starry good that comes to me.

I stick with whatever I set my mind to, and I persevere.

I am filled with self-worth, I have stardust in my veins. The moon shines for me tonight, and self-love is my right.

My intuition guides me, and it feels right.

I am healthy and happy.

I am excited for my journey, and the new me I am becoming.

I encourage myself every day, because I can do it. I AM doing it.

It's time for sleep, and it's time for release. Good-bye, _____.

I close my eyes and slide effortlessly into a deep, healing sleep.

Pillow Self-Talk Mantra

Choose one of the following. (See instructions, Chapter 5.)

- *I release _____ from my life forever.*
- *I am powerful. I am the master of my mind.*
- *I love me. I am worthy.*

SCRIPT: COPING WITH GRIEF

Perhaps they are not stars, but rather openings in heaven where the love of our lost ones pours through and shines down upon us to let us know they are happy.

— INUIT PROVERB

Life is a cycle.

Sometimes traumatic events happen. That's a normal part of the cycle of life. Your new, empowered and loving mindset will help you navigate these with grace.

Grief is a completely natural response to loss. It can appear in different life situations: grief from losing a loved one or a pet to death, grief from losing someone to a breakup, grief from losing an opportunity, or losing a familiar or cherished way of life.

You can even grieve over lost time. When I learned the power of self-love and self-worth, and I realized how much of my life had been spent in needless pain, I grieved over the years I had lost, during which, I could have been so much happier.

Grief is an emotion that needs to be processed. The best way to do that is through lots of self-love and patience. You don't want to ignore grief or suppress it. You want to process it. When you step into your own power, knowing that you can handle grief, your courage is sparked, like the first star that comes out in the night sky. This confidence in yourself brings you some peace, and this peace helps you navigate your way back to joy.

Sometimes, the grief can reappear at unexpected times, and that's ok. That's natural. Let the grief work its way through you, as you breathe deep breaths of peace back into your soul.

Remember... life is a cycle. There's an energy to life, a natural ebb and flow. It makes you grow.

No matter the cause of one's grief, when losing something, it can hurt. We feel the lack, as though lack were an actual thing. The more we cling to someone or something, the deeper the sense of loss. We feel attached to loved ones, and we experience grief as a result of not having them in our lives anymore. And this is part of life, loving hard, loving with all our heart. It's a beautiful thing to love so much. But just because they're not here physically, does not mean you can't feel their energy and still smile at the memories and speak to them.

My husband and I are very close. My mom and I are, too. I've long since known that, if there is a time when I'm still walking on this earth and they aren't, they will be floating next to me. And you can be sure I'll be talking to them, looking for signs of them hearing me and communicating back.

I think of the lyrics in the song, *Birds*, by Imagine Dragons...

When the moon is lookin' down

Shinin' light upon your ground

I'm flyin' up to let you see

That the shadow cast is me.

All people, plants, and animals have energy. It's there with or without a physical body. Our souls will always glow. If you're in a place of grieving right now, then tonight's Pillow Self-Talk is meant for you. To begin, be gentle with yourself, and love yourself. That's the place to start. Know that you will, in time, process your grief, and eventually replace the pain with feelings of pure love. If you believe this now, you can have more peace through this process.

Pillow Self-Talk Script: Coping with Grief

I love myself so very, very much, and I am gentle with myself during this precious time.

I have peace and calm all around me, and I can lean into it anytime.

There are cycles in all of life... the years, the seasons, the moon. Cycles are natural, and I take comfort in knowing this.

I live, I grow, I glow. I allow myself to feel my grief, and then, when I'm ready, I let go.

I am gentle with myself as I process this experience and these feelings. I am love, and I am loved.

I feel what I need to feel, and then I love myself and let it go. I open my beautiful hands and release it back to the universe.

I speak lovingly to myself, about myself, and about my life.

I'm worthy. I'm worthy. I'm worthy.

I feel peaceful thoughts for the cycle of life, and I honor it.

I take comfort in the memories of my loved one.

The cells in my body are aglow with peace.

I make choices that are deeply loving. I recognize painful moments, but I know they will pass. I am full of love.

I take deep, relaxed breaths. I take my time. I feel peace.

I am creating a life I love.

I move through the world, open to help, and it's a beautiful feeling.

I am energy, I flow. My spirit is here. I feel it and glow.

I hold on to the beautiful love, and I release the grief. It's all good. All is well.

Every night, it becomes a little bit easier. I am relaxed. I am whole.

I allow myself space between the stories of my life.

I align myself with peace.

Life is a continuous process, and I persevere, honoring the journey with love and strength.

I move through life from a place of calm, and I am happy, wherever I am.

The world is a living force, pulsing with love, and it wraps me in a warm embrace that feels good.

I am gentle and patient with myself as I heal, because I am worthy.

Miracles constantly arrive in my life, and my needs are always met.

I am ever-changing, ever-spinning, ever-slow-dancing with my soul.

Pillow Self-Talk Mantra

Choose one of the following. (See instructions, Chapter 5.)

- *I hold love in my soul.*
- *I love myself.*
- *I breathe in peace.*

SCRIPT: PROFOUND PEACE

I love the night. It's not unusual for me to see the light of a new day before closing my eyes on the old one.

— Peggy Toney Horton

This Pillow Self-Talk script is all about feeling peace. It's about embracing a relaxed and peaceful attitude about life, and love, and feeling peace, because you know your dreams and goals are coming to you. Even in your sleep.

Expectation of success brings a sense of peace when you're wanting to manifest an incredible life, full of abundance, health, and success. If you ever have moments of worry, about whether this manifesting stuff will work for you, then rest easy, and feel peaceful that it will.

As I mentioned in Chapter 3, I call this *Happy Expectation*.

When you do the work... thinking and feeling elevated thoughts and feelings, taking inspired action, loving yourself and your life, then you set yourself up for huge success. Know it with confidence. It's coming. Believe in it. Believe in you. That's your job... *take the plunge,* and then let the current carry you. That will bring you peace. The Happy Expectation.

And that elevated feeling draws your dreams closer to you.

If you have a particular situation in life where you want more peace, then take a moment to turn up your self-love and confidence. Peace is there for the taking, waiting for you to grab it. You are worthy of peace. Go ahead and let go of anything interfering with your peace, and relax. Think and feel good things, and let the Universe do the rest by bringing you inspired ideas in the night.

Pillow Self-Talk Script: Profound Peace with Happy Expectation

The stillness of the evening is deep and soothing.

I have peace in all areas of my life. Soothing peace wraps around my shoulders like a warm, plush blanket.

I love life, and life loves me. I live with Happy Expectation.

I am worthy of peace, and it is easy for me to let go when I need to let go.

I am calm. So very, very calm.

Relaxation is the key to manifestation.

I rest easy every night when my head sinks into my pillow, because I come from a place of powerful peace and Happy Expectation. I believe in the process. I believe in me.

The planets spin and dance with the stars. It's profoundly peaceful and magical. I will join them when my eyes close.

The world is so big, and this idea expands my feelings and ideas. I'm filled with awe. I am never alone.

When I open my eyes every morning, I know I'm going to have an amazing day, filled with love and peace.

Health surrounds me, and fills me at all times. I love taking care of myself.

I close my eyes and breathe in harmony.

My heart is peace. My brain is tranquil. My soul rests with ease.

I'm so confident. I'm full of love. I rise, and rise, and rise, up to the starry sky above. I dance on moonbeams. My spirit flies.

I love being present, and it's soothing. I glow with peace, and I have time to just be.

I float amongst the rainbow clouds of life, with my arms open, my hands-free, and peace tingles in my fingers. My heart pumps with ease. I love me.

I flow from a place of ease and effortlessness. Kindness surrounds me.

My life is full of magic and full of love. I love myself. All is well.

As I fall asleep, I have inner peace. Yes, as I fall asleep, I have inner peace, full of Happy Expectation.

Pillow Self-Talk Mantra

Choose one of the following. (See instructions, Chapter 5.)

- *I glow with peace.*
- *I love life, and life loves me.*
- *I have Happy Expectation. All is well.*

ETERNAL HAPPINESS

Happiness is one of the easiest ways to manifest a magical life, because when you have pure happiness, you *feeeeel magical,* and your elevated emotional state attracts your dreams and desires to you. It's like floating, it's like starlight and rocket ship rides, it's shooting stars, full moons, and the *feeling of living in a fairytale.*

And here, too... sleep is instrumental. If you're low on quality sleep, your emotions become erratic. But fear not... *Dreams to the rescue!* Dream sleep, specifically, soothes your emotional state and supports a calm, relaxed mindset.

This section includes the following Pillow Self-Talk scripts for *Eternal Happiness***:**

- *Hoppin' Happiness*
- *I'm a Cool, Calm Cat*
- *Seeing Silver Linings*
- *Stellar Sleep & Dreams*
- *Dance with the Universe*

SCRIPT: HOPPIN' HAPPINESS

Life is the night sky.

All the dots of stars are happiness.

— RICHARD L. RATLIFF

For just a moment, think about your favorite things. The things that bring you joy. Is it lovely weather? Puppies? Funny cats? The feel of your young child's or grandchild's hand in yours? Feel that gentle happiness stir inside you. Maybe it's thinking about how happy you are to be sliding into bed and relaxing.

Maybe it's chocolate! Or, coffee... of course. *Mmm... so nice.*

Here is a delightful little script about happiness, because we are all happier when feeling and thinking about happy things. Open your heart, expand your soul, and widen your mind to *all things happy*. Sometimes, if I have an off day, I simply repeat in my mind the mantra, *"I am happy. I am happy. I am happy,"* and things start to feel better. I'm still amazed that this works, but it does.

Go ahead and bliss out. It's time.

Pillow Self-Talk Script: Hoppin' Happiness

I am happy.

I love being happy, and I am worthy of happiness.

I love my life. I have time to just be. To be blissfully happy.

I am unconditional happiness. I easily align myself with a happy feeling.

I am happy wherever I am, glittering with gratitude. Thank you, Life. Thank you, Me.

It is safe to follow my truth. My heart is safe.

Bliss sparkles all around me, all over me, and all through me. Sparkle, sparkle, sparkle.

I love happiness, and happiness loves me.

Abundance is everywhere I turn. It is all around me. It's here, it's there, it's everywhere. I am blessed.

Bliss, joy, and happiness are words I use every day. The more often I use them, the more often I feel them.

Happiness is fun, and I look forward to feeling happy every day.

I reach up into the night sky, it's open and wide, mystical and alive. I fill it with my dreams, and it relaxes me with peace.

Kitty cats, puppy dogs, and roses in bloom. I love them all.

I am happy, and this makes me healthy. Happiness heals.

As I rest my eyes tonight, I enter a beautiful state of dreaming, filled with happiness.

Blissful, colorful dreams are coming to me right now.

I tilt my head up to the night sky, full of worthiness, attracting all of my desires to me. I wake up in the morning, looking forward to my day, with boundless appreciation for this rainbow way.

I am wild with happiness.

My imagination is powerful. When I think and feel uplifted, with my arms wide open, it brings an avalanche of happiness to me.

Every day, I experience an intense degree of excitement and awe. I am the master of my life.

The adventures of my dreams await me in the silvery moonlight.

I am my own happy place. Stars, glitter, rainbows, and waves.

It's time to rest my head now, and slip into my beautiful dreamland. The colors of the night soothe me as I fall asleep. Good night.

Pillow Self-Talk Mantra

Choose one of the following. (See instructions, Chapter 5.)

- *I am happy. I am happy. I am happy.*
- *I sparkle with joy.*
- *My heart is safe and loved.*

SCRIPT: I'M A COOL, CALM CAT

Learn to be calm, and you will always be happy.

— PARAMAHANSA YOGANANDA

Tonight's Pillow Self-Talk was inspired by the children's book, *Pete the Cat*, which I love. It's about Pete the Cat and his nice, new white shoes.

I remember reading this book to my daughter when she was young, and we'd fall into fits of giggles. The message was so good. This cat, Pete, has his white shoes, and he loves them. But as he wears the shoes and walks through life, they change colors because he steps in different things.

They're no longer white.

But he doesn't mind.

He keeps "walking along and singing his song."

I love this metaphor. You can wear *white shoes*, and get them dirty, and it can be upsetting, or it can be playful and fun. My family used Pete as an example for all kinds of things. If I dropped a jar of jelly, and it went splat all over the Mexican tile floor, my daughter would yell from her room, *"Be like Pete the Cat, Mom!"*

And it worked.

I'd chill out, relax, and clean up the mess. My floor probably needed to be cleaned anyway.

Whatever happens in life, I encourage you to embrace an *I'm a cool, calm cat* attitude. I promise, there are *always* silver linings in life's experiences—even if you can't see them in the moment. Over time, they will shine. And if you keep telling yourself *I'm a cool, calm cat,* you'll quickly start to be just that.

Pillow Self-Talk Script: I'm a Cool, Calm Cat

I'm a cool, calm cat, and life is fun for me.

I sing my song, no matter what is going on, and life is fun for me.

I have the most amazing dreams, full of splashy color, because life is fun for me.

What resonates with me will always find me.

I'm a cool calm cat, and I am relaxed.

I flow through life, easy-breezy, and this makes life playful and easy.

I'm a cool calm cat, and I make my dreams come true.

Gems of possibility catch my eye. I find them everywhere, sparkling just for me.

I am all the colors of the rainbow, at all different days and times. I love my versatility.

Being a cool, calm cat makes me laugh at all kinds of things.

I can be a cool, calm cat anytime I want. Cats are cool, I am cool, and life is way more fun this way.

I create energy with my words and manifest my dreams with this frequency. Adaptability is my superpower.

The key to realizing my dreams is to achieve a vibrational connection with that which I desire, like a lock and a key—ka-chunk. Life is fun for me.

I allow the process to unfold, and I am relaxed and open. I am kind, and I am bold.

I am falling asleep with calming thoughts, and my body relaxes in peace. Did ya know? I'm a cool calm cat.

I remain focused on what matters: happiness, joy, and me.

When I am happy and peaceful, I see more happy and peaceful things. I choose my focus. It's my privilege. It's my responsibility.

Tonight is all that matters. Right here, right now. I'm ready for deep sleep tonight.

I breathe easy through all hours of the day, and all hours of the night. In and out. In and out.

My body is healthy, calm, and happy. Prosperity is all around me.

I am lovable and cuddly. Life is so very, very good.

The stars will come out tonight, I'll get my best sleep. I tuck myself in with love, and I breathe with ease.

Thank you, night. I'm ready to dream.

Pillow Self-Talk Mantra

Choose one of the following. (See instructions, Chapter 5.)

- *I'm a cool, calm cat.*
- *Life is easy and breezy.*
- *I am resting into the night, and it feels so right.*

SCRIPT: SEEING SILVER LININGS

The air is of silver and pearl, the night is liquid with moonlight.

— WILLA CATHER

Seeing the good in situations is similar to being the *cool, calm cat* that I wrote about in the previous script. Seeing the good imbues a divine vibe, colored in relaxation, knowing, and forever calm. It's a way of life.

If you think about your day today, and if you experienced anything challenging, or unexpected, or less than ideal, then you can respond by simply being *a cool, calm cat*. And also... by seeing the good in it.

Revel in the silver lining.

It's always there.

There will inevitably be profound good in everything that happens. Even tragedy, because we grow from it. It's like a law of nature, a law of life. *It's the rainbow after the rain.*

We all know the expression, *Every cloud has a silver lining*. And as a generally positive person, I had always believed it, more or less. But I really began taking the expression seriously when I became a novelist. Every less-than-ideal thing that happened in my life suddenly provided me with material to include in my writing. From minor mishaps, to unpleasant people, to major challenges... it all informed my storytelling and added color and texture to my characters. It's all grist for the mill.

And not just the occasional thing here and there. No, *every single thing that happens in my life, becomes part of my own story.*

This is true for everyone, not just novelists.

These events are a large part of what makes up *your story*. In fact, over time, you'll find that these are actually what makes life most interesting. Sure, the wins and funny stuff are nice too, but half of the crappiest stuff in life ends up being funny later. You know the saying, "Someday, we'll look back at this and laugh"... well, sometimes *someday* is literally just hours later.

Whether humorous or not, the trick is to train your brain to embrace it all. Instead of getting upset, stressed, or irritated, make your default mindset instead say, *"This might be less than ideal now, but this will be a good story later!"*

Once this attitude became my norm, I was hooked.

And even if you don't care about stories, life's events still become *experience*, and that is where you get *wisdom*. And wisdom helps you live a better life going forward.

This also means you can share your wisdom with other people, which is a profound and beautiful benefit for all.

So now, my default is *always to see the good. See the Silver Linings.*

In all people.

In all situations.

Pillow Self-Talk Script: Seeing Silver Linings

Thank you, Life, for today.

I am falling asleep with loving thoughts and feelings. Life is full of silver linings.

I'm brilliant, and I love to learn from life's lessons. I am strong. I am courageous. I am a star, shining in the black night sky, lighting my own way.

There is no one else in the world like me. I'm me, and I love me.

I'm living a completely new life of my own creative design. I am grateful.

I am full of optimism, and I am passionate about living my destiny.

I support others with love and kindness.

I can always find the good in things. The treasures in Life's Flow. I'm a treasure hunter. It's fun, and I am bold and adventurous.

I am in the right place, at the right time, doing the right thing.

I might not have all the answers, but I'm open to life's brilliant unfolding. I ease my mind into the night.

I move through the world, and through life, from a place of love. Deep, deep, soul-stirring love.

I am the standard by which I measure my worth, and I am so very worthy.

Miracles and twinkling synchronicities always find me. My needs are always met. All is always well.

I embrace all of my uniqueness—I'm magical.

With quality sleep, I show up better to my life.

I believe in me. I believe in possibility!

I am generous.

I am receptive to how the night unfolds for me.

Patience. Beautiful stardust. A night full of open space for my dreams to uncoil, unravel, unbend, and come true, as my thoughts relax. As I glide silently into the night.

I am rich with thankfulness for my mindset of living, loving, and seeing the brilliance in Life's Flow. It always benefits me.

It is only in the dark of the night when I can see the stars. I am honored to dance with life.

All is well.

Whenever I look for the good in situations, it makes me happy and filled with peace. I love the stars, because they are the lightness and sparkling beauty in the darkness.

My love for myself grows every night, more and more.

Pillow Self-Talk Mantra

Choose one of the following. (See instructions, Chapter 5.)

- *I love learning from life.*
- *I grow from my experiences, like a sprout from a seed.*
- *There is always good to be found.*

SCRIPT: STELLAR SLEEP & DREAMS

There is nothing like a dream to create the future.

— VICTOR HUGO

If you ever have difficulty falling asleep, then tonight's script is for you. It's filled with lines that are relaxing, and they direct your brain to get tired and ready for a stellar sleep and incredible dreams. As you know by now, sleep is an integral part to living your legendary life, so making sleep a priority is an easy win.

Pillow Self-Talk Script: Stellar Sleep & Dreams

I love the night. It is magical and calming.

The moon will guide me through the night with her beautiful brightness as I sleep and dream.

I am getting sleepy and ready for a profoundly deep, deep sleep.

I let go of the past... I'm not attached to it. I love to learn from life and move on.

I respect myself, and I get a proper night's sleep to support me. Deep sleep is coming.

The evening is twinkling with optimism and peace, and I rest easy. I am sleepy.

I fall asleep in the embrace of dreams, in the welcoming arms of the night.

I am sleepy, and my eyes are getting heavy. It feels good to close them and rest.

I create a lovely energy with my imagination, and this brings me dreams that fill my sleep with magic.

I surrender to the sublime. My shoulders and back relax. I uncurl my toes. I lie back.

My life is unfolding beautifully, and I am destined for golden greatness. I focus on what I love, and this draws it to me.

Relaxation flows through my veins, and it feels soooo good. Sleep beckons me.

The darkness of night brings solitude. My body is ready for a full rest.

I'm an intuitive manifester. It's fun tapping into my intuition for guidance. It will drive my dreams tonight. Deep sleep is coming.

I have amazing strength for any situation, and knowing that, I rest tonight in peace.

I attract fantastical dreams steeped in deep color, and I am grateful for the calm in my life. I feel it right here, right now.

My rich, warm dreams are coming to me as I fall into restful sleep. Shhhhh.

I am grateful for my bed, my pillow, and the rich darkness of the night. Shhhhh.

I fan my dreams with fire and love. I close my eyes, ready for sleep. Shhhhh.

Pillow Self-Talk Mantra

Choose one of the following. (See instructions, Chapter 5.)

- *I am sleepy and full of peace.*
- *I get the best sleep.*
- *My body is relaxed. I am relaxed.*

SCRIPT: DANCE WITH THE UNIVERSE

Night quilts the sky with stars sewn like the uneven stitching of my jacket.

— ALEXANDRA CHRISTO

One of my favorite parts of living this amazing life is *dancing with the universe*. Twirling round and round with *Life's Magical Flow*. Because this life you live is *a dance*. We are partners with our creation, with Life, with the Universe—through our energy. When you walk through life with your arms wide open, with beautiful expectancy because of your effusive self-worth, manifesting your dreams becomes so *natural*. So expected.

You have the world in your hands.

The universe conspires to help you. It's only strange when you don't listen, so stop hitting the snooze button every time the Universe taps you on the shoulder. Let yourself be guided to the perfect solutions, the golden opportunities, and your expansive dream life, because they're headed your way. Be open and honest, and move through the world from a place of love, and eventually, the ego's overzealous drive to control everything crumbles away and is replaced with a relaxed openness to all the answers you need.

Allow this process to happen. Open your mind to the mysterious. Be quiet, listen to the Universe, and receive its guidance.

This final Pillow Self-Talk script is filled with lines of self-talk that create a sense of awe and wonder as you fall into blissful sleep.

Sweet dreams.

Pillow Self-Talk Script: Dance with the Universe

The stars wink at me, and I wink back. We dance together, and I know the secret to life is all about the magical energy of love.

I am available for anything that comes to me in my dreams and in my life, including that which seems beyond imagining. I am ready. Bring it on.

I twirl with bright strings of stars—dancing, smiling, and playing with the Universe.

I glow with the enthusiasm of success. I am worthy.

I have a love for the marvelous, and I believe in possibilities. They buzz all around me.

I am bursting with delight as I dance with life.

I'm grateful for my connection to the channels of Flow.

I take a long, soft, deep breath, and the sweet evening energy suffuses my body. I am relaxed. I am ethereal. I am magical.

I'm always learning and growing. I love how I think and feel. I love the power I have to design the life I want.

I am building my dreams into my reality, and Life's Flow supports my every move. I love the magic of life and all of its vast possibilities.

My life gets more fabulous every day. I look forward to what each new sunrise brings. Life's adventures await me.

I move freely, and I go places and have wonderful experiences. I have freedom and ease of schedule, and I enjoy my moments and my time. I am blessed. I am fortune. I am love.

I was born knowing my way. I close my eyes and reconnect with my sparkling self now.

I attract great things easily. I am lucky.

I am transforming into something new and wonderful. I embrace my power.

I am the master of my mind. I choose my focus. I love.

I'm a supernova! Awesome ideas are exploding into existence all around me, coming to me in my sleep.

I light up the world with my song.

I am inspired by nature, by the moon, the planets, and the stars. I relax into the night as it wraps its arms around me. All is well. All is right.

Pillow Self-Talk Mantra

Choose one of the following. (See instructions, Chapter 5.)

- *I dance with the Universe.*
- *All is always well.*
- *I feel complete peace. It's all around me.*

NEXT STEPS & FREE BONUS SCRIPTS

I am excited that you've finished this book! Thank you for joining me on this adventure. And remember, when you are making changes in your life, *you have to show up to get the results*. With this ritual, it'll be easy, and so enjoyable. So peaceful and relaxing. Get ready to look forward to bedtime like never before.

Free Bonus Scripts

Shoot me an email to receive a free PDF with three bonus Pillow Self-Talk scripts:

- *The Magic of Life*
- *Soaring Confidence*
- *It's Coming to Me (Abundance)*

Email me at:

Kristen@KristenHelmstetter.com

Please specify that you'd like the "*Pillow Self-Talk goodies*."

∾

I have a HUGE favor to ask of you.

If you would help me, I'd greatly appreciate it. I'd love it if you would leave a review for this *Pillow Self-Talk* book on Amazon. Reviews are incredibly important for authors, and I'm extremely grateful if you could write one!

∾

I'd love to hear from you! Email me at:

Kristen@KristenHelmstetter.com

Or find me at: Instagram.com/coffeeselftalk

Podcast

You can hear me on the *Coffee Self-Talk with Kristen Helmstetter* podcast wherever you listen to podcasts or at:

https://anchor.fm/kristen-helmstetter

And come join our fun and lively group for readers:

Facebook.com/groups/coffeeselftalk

∾

What's Next?

Here are the other books in the Coffee Self-Talk family:

International Bestseller – Over 150,000 Copies Sold

Coffee Self-Talk: 5 Minutes a Day to Start Living Your Magical Life

Coffee Self-Talk is a powerful, life-changing routine that takes only 5 minutes a day. What if you could wake up every morning feeling more incredible than ever before... in 5 minutes? **Living the most epic life. Your mind mastered!** Coffee Self-Talk transforms your life by boosting your self-esteem, filling you with happiness, and helping you attract the magical life you dream of living. *All this, with your next cup of coffee.*

The Coffee Self-Talk Daily Reader #1:

Bite-Sized Nuggets of Magic to Add to Your Morning Ritual

This companion book offers short, daily reads for tips and inspiration. It does not replace your daily Coffee Self-Talk routine. Rather, it's meant to be used each day *after* you do your Coffee Self-Talk.

If you do one reading per day, it will take 30 days to complete.

KRISTEN HELMSTETTER

TEA TIME SELF-TALK

a little afternoon bliss
for living your magical life

by the bestselling author of
COFFEE SELF-TALK

Tea Time Self-Talk:

A Little Afternoon Bliss for Living Your Magical Life

The perfect 5-minute, afternoon break companion, designed to give you a blissful moment to yourself for reflection and motivation.

KRISTEN HELMSTETTER

WINE SELF-TALK™

15 minutes
to relax &
tap into
your inner
genius

by the bestselling author of
COFFEE SELF-TALK™

Wine Self-Talk:

15 Minutes to Relax & Tap Into Your Inner Genius

There is a source of sacred wisdom in you. *Wine Self-Talk* is a simple,
delicious ritual to help you relax, unwind, and tap into your inner genius.

KRISTEN HELMSTETTER

COFFEE SELF-TALK ™

GUIDED JOURNAL

Writing Prompts &
Inspiration for Living
Your Magical Life

The Coffee Self-Talk Guided Journal:

Writing Prompts & Inspiration for Living Your Magical Life

This guided journal keeps you *lit up and glowing* as you go deeper into your magical Coffee Self-Talk journey. Experience the joy of journaling, mixed with fun, thought-provoking exercises, and discover hidden gems about yourself. Get inspired, slash your anxiety, and unleash your amazing, badass self.

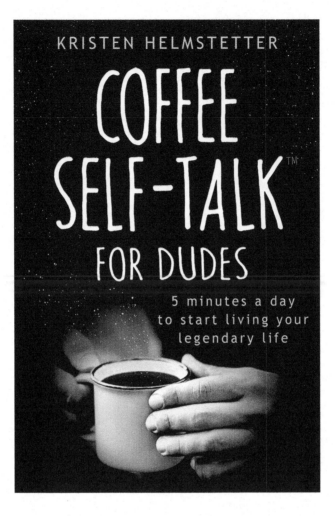

Coffee Self-Talk for Dudes:

5 Minutes a Day to Start Living Your Legendary Life

This is a special edition of *Coffee Self-Talk* that has been edited to be more oriented toward men in the language, examples, and scripts. It is 95% identical to the original *Coffee Self-Talk* book.

Coffee Self-Talk for Teen Girls:

5 Minutes a Day for Confidence, Achievement & Lifelong Happiness

This is written for girls in high school (ages 13 to 17). It covers the same ideas as *Coffee Self-Talk*, and applies them to the issues that teen girls face, such as school, grades, sports, peer pressure, social media, social anxiety, beauty/body issues, and dating.

Made in the USA
Middletown, DE
20 September 2022

10863290R00126